Teaching Hispanic Children

Teaching Hispanic Children

Toni Griego Jones
University of Arizona

Mary Lou Fuller
Professor Emeritus
University of North Dakota

Boston New York San Francisco
Mexico City Montreal Toronto London Madrid Munich Paris
Hong Kong Singapore Tokyo Cape Town Sydney

Series Editor: *Traci Mueller*
Editorial Assistant: *Erica Tromblay*
Marketing Manager: *Amy Cronin*
Editorial-Production Service: *Omegatype Typography, Inc.*
Manufacturing Buyer: *Andrew Turso*
Composition Buyer: *Linda Cox*
Cover Administrator: *Kristina Mose-Libon*
Electronic Composition: *Omegatype Typography, Inc.*

For related titles and support materials, visit our online catalog at www.ablongman.com.

Library of Congress Cataloging-in-Publication Data

Jones, Toni Griego.
Teaching Hispanic children / Toni Griego Jones, Mary Lou Fuller.
p. cm.
Includes bibliographical references and index.
ISBN 0-205-32530-0
1. Hispanic American children—Education. 2. Hispanic American children—Social conditions. 3. Language and education—United States. I. Fuller, Mary Lou. II. Title.

LC2669 .J66 2003
317.829'68073—dc21

2002074773

Printed in the United States of America

10 9 8 7 6 5 4 3 2 1 07 06 05 04 03 02

The children and teachers I have worked with over the years have inspired and encouraged me to write about my experiences in teaching and teacher education. I thank them for their support and advocacy in improving education for Hispanic children. In Latino fashion, I also thank my entire family and dedicate this book to them, especially to my grandparents who valued education above all else, to my son, and to my mother who always taught us to respect and value ourselves and every other human being. Thanks also to Lillie Manson, teacher educator at the University of Arizona, for her thoughtfull review of our manuscript.

—Toni Griego Jones

I have been inspired by more people than I can ever thank. However, the following four were particularly influential in motivating me to speak out for a better education for an often neglected group of children. And so I dedicate this book to them:

Dr. Luis Casuas (Professor Emeritus, Highlands University) for his guidance and encouragement in the study of Hispanic families.

Dr. Mary Harris (Former Dean of the Center for Teaching and Learning at the University of North Dakota) for both her belief in multicultural education and (more importantly) for her active support of the integration of the study of diversity into undergraduate and graduate education programs.

Dr. Carl Grant (Professor, University of Wisconsin at Madison) for his scholarship and leadership in the area of multiculturalism, and for his accessibility to those of us who share his enthusiasm for work in that area.

Dr. Hank Slotnick (Visiting Professor, University of Wisconsin, and my husband), for his patience, and his continuing and unconditional support.

—Mary Lou Fuller

CONTENTS

PREFACE

Our children are worth a little care...they are uncut diamonds, but no one wants to bother to dig for them and polish them.

—Hispanic mother talking about
Hispanic students in Arizona

Over the last several years, we've had the opportunity to interview Mexican American parents about what they think should be in teacher education programs to prepare teachers to be more effective with their children. A recurring theme in those interviews was the hope that new teachers would care about their children and would take the time to find out about their homes, their neighborhoods, and cultural backgrounds. Parents know that their children are bright, talented, and capable of learning. One Mexican American mother captured the sentiment with the words at the beginning of this preface, comparing the children to rough, uncut "diamonds," vibrant and full of energy, intelligence, and warmth. But she worried, and we worry too, that not enough of the teaching force is ready to polish these children, to bring them to their full potential.

We agree there is a treasure ready to be discovered and polished in American public schools today and that there is a spark just waiting to be struck between teachers who care and Hispanic students who are longing to be cared for. Following are our assumptions in writing this book:

- Teachers and prospective teachers care about all children, including Hispanic children.
- Teachers have a desire to teach all children, including Hispanic children.
- Teachers are interested in knowing more about how to be successful with all the children entrusted to them, including Hispanic children.

The history of schooling for Hispanic and other minority groups in the United States has not always been a success story. Some groups have benefitted from the educational system and others, primarily racial and ethnic minorities, have been excluded or have not done well in our schools. Teachers and preservice teachers need to understand these histories and backgrounds to understand their students' attitudes toward schools as well as to understand their academic situation. We also assume that teachers and prospective teachers *want* to improve the U.S. system of education to make it work for all groups.

Teachers often say that all children are the same, that children all have the same basic needs regardless of their cultural backgrounds, and that teachers treat all children the same. It is true that all humans have the same basic physical and emotional needs, but in denying the importance of cultural differences, we basically deny the individuality of each of our students as well. People are products of their cultural groups, and in a society as culturally diverse as that of the United States, educators need to recognize differences in the ways children are socialized. The Hispanic population itself is very diverse, depending on a variety of factors, including national origin, time in this country, geographical region, income level, and age. Teachers need to recognize those differences within the Hispanic population as well, but it is not possible to deal with each Hispanic population within the confines of this book. Because the Mexican American population is not only the largest but also the most widely distributed geographically, we focused on this population to discuss points in each chapter. Unless there is a determined understanding across all cultural groups, there will likely be misunderstandings based on false assumptions about people from different cultural backgrounds.

The target of this book is teachers, those who are in initial teacher preparation programs and those already in schools. The book is full of information about Hispanic populations, but the focus is on the teacher and what teachers should know and understand to teach Hispanic students effectively. The idea is to help connect teachers and Hispanic students. We believe that teacher preparation needs to be discussed in relation to all racial and ethnic groups so that teachers can maximize the achievement of every student. In the case of Hispanic student populations, the need to understand and attend to them is particularly urgent for reasons important to society in the United States, not just to individual Hispanic students. These reasons are:

1. At the start of the millenium, Hispanics are the largest minority group in the United States at 12.4 percent of the student population.
2. They have a disproportionate, chronic record of underachievement and high drop out rates in U.S. schools.
3. Hispanic underachievement places the social and economic welfare of the nation at risk. When a sizeable group is undereducated and there is such disparity between groups, there is risk to the entire society, not just to one group or to individuals.

We hope that readers of this book will consider three aspects of U.S. public schools and make a meaningful connection among them. The first of the three aspects is the demographic composition of U.S. public school teachers. In 2000, the composition of the teaching force in the United States was 87 percent white, middle class and 74 percent female. This is not likely to change in the next millenium, as racial and ethnic minorities are not entering the teaching profession at a rate that approximates the student populations. In fact, the numbers of minority teachers are declining each year. In the 1970s and 1980s, following the Civil Rights Movement, there was a short period of increase in the numbers of racial/ethnic minority teachers, but in the 1990s there were fewer minorities going into teaching.

The second aspect of public schools to consider is the composition of the student population. This population is increasingly nonwhite, from racial and ethnic minority groups. Of the 51 million students in U.S. schools in 1997, 35 percent were from minority groups and by 2000, that number rose to 40 percent. In urban areas and certain regions, racial and ethnic minorities make up the majority of student populations. In all the largest cities, racial and ethnic minorities are the majority student populations. Clearly, the composition of the teaching force differs dramatically from the composition of the student populations. In this book we address the implications of this difference from the perspective of the Hispanic population, but many of the same points may apply to other racial and ethnic minority groups.

The third and perhaps most important fact about public schools is that, for the most part, teachers and Hispanic students are not making a successful connection in U.S. public schools. Although there are individual exceptions, Hispanic students overall are not successful in U.S. schools. Stated another way, public schools are failing to educate Hispanic students. There is a tragic disconnect between two critical groups in the educational enterprise—the teaching force and Hispanic student populations. In schools that are predominantly Hispanic and in schools where there are only a few, the disconnect seems pervasive, as indicated by the dropout rates and academic underachievement of Hispanic students overall.

Chapter 1 discusses the importance of addressing the education of Hispanic students and gives an overview of demographics. It presents information about the role of national origins and cultural background in teaching and learning and why it is important for teachers to know about culture in general, and about Hispanic cultural groups in particular. The second chapter focuses on the need for educators to understand their own thinking about Hispanic populations, to reflect on their knowledge, attitudes, and beliefs about populations that have long been part of the American landscape, but are now becoming a more visible part of it. The theme of reflection is carried throughout each chapter with questions that will guide the reader to reflect on the content of the chapter and on the implications for themselves as professional educators. Rather than focus on providing tips and strategies that may last only a few days, we attempted to have the reader focus on the points of the chapters through reflective exercises at the end of most chapters. The intent is for teachers (preservice and inservice) to begin developing their own methods and approaches to connecting with Hispanic students in their own situations once they have a better understanding of their own relationship with Hispanic students. Instead of reinventing effective practices, we included many references to existing resources, highlighting our own favorites. We often wrote in the first person, describing and reflecting on our own experience as teacher educators. Sometimes these reflections are highighted in boxed areas as Author's Notes.

The history and background chapters on culture and language provide knowledge and a deeper understanding of the lives of Hispanic children in the United States and help teachers and prospective teachers expand their professional perspectives. In writing the chapters on classroom practice and how to work with family and parents, we have tried to directly address points identified in educational literature as effective practices for Hispanic children.

The dramatic increase in Hispanic school-age populations and the resultant necessity to do a better job educating these children can be approached as a problem or as an exciting new era in public schooling. If teachers accept the challenge of polishing those "uncut diamonds," they can make a difference for the nation and for individuals. Even though one teacher cannot change the world or stem the tide of large-scale failure, one teacher can make a difference for the Hispanic children who live for a time in his or her classroom. It has been too easy to focus on the negative, to think only of the difficulties in preparing all teachers to be effective teachers of Hispanic children. We must deliberately seek research, not only on effective classroom practices for Hispanic students, but equally important, on effective practices in preparing teachers to teach Hispanic students. The practice of reflecting on our own beliefs and knowledge about the cultural backgrounds of all students is one that holds a great deal of promise.

Acknowledgments

We would like to thank the reviewer for this edition: Dr. Susan McIntyre, University of Wisconsin.

ABOUT THE AUTHORS

Improving the instruction of Hispanic children is the responsibility and privilege of all educators. With this in mind, we share with you our insights, expertise, and experiences. By bringing our common interests and differing backgrounds to this task, we hope to contribute to your understanding of how to approach educating this growing and important school population.

Mary Lou Fuller, Ph.D.

I am like most teachers of Hispanic students in that I am a white, non-Hispanic female. My demographic status means that I, as other non-Hispanic educators, must continually learn about this group, both formally and informally. I have been an elementary classroom teacher, a school psychologist, and for twenty years, a professor at the University of North Dakota. Though I now hold emerita status there, I am an adjunct faculty member at Northern Arizona University. All these varieties of educational experiences have contributed to the reasons I care so deeply about the topic of this book.

With the exception of the time I spent teaching on the Navajo Reservation, I have always had Hispanic children in my elementary classrooms. This was the case regardless of whether my school was in a small, isolated mountain town in New Mexico, or any of the four Arizona communities where I lived and taught. Students in my classes were as widely varied as the Hispanic population itself: high and low SES, children who spoke English as either a native or second language, children from families that were very traditional and those from highly acculturated homes, and children who excelled in school and those who struggled—and occasionally failed. The insights I gained from working with these children and their families illuminate the ideas and suggestions you'll find in the pages of this book.

What did I learn from these classroom experiences? I learned that at its heart, the elementary curriculum was designed for white middle-class students, and that the presence of children from different cultures and economic groups was generally not considered in developing the curriculum. Put simply, varying cultures and economic circumstances were not recognized and even less often appreciated. Nevertheless, Hispanic children were expected to learn from a curriculum and be evaluated using procedures that didn't make a lot of sense for children who didn't share experiences with those coming from White, middle class homes.

I came to understand better the implications of the lack of fit between the needs of Hispanic children and the elementary curriculum when I became a school psychologist, especially in the area of assessment. I came to see that because both achievement and intelligence tests have questions that require an understanding of middle-class experiences and sensibilities, the question was less a test of achievement or intelligence and more a test of degree of assimilation. This being the case, and because such tests do not consider degree of acculturation into the middle class as a variable, achievement tests too often became self-fulfilling prophecies about under-achievement, and intelligence tests became life sentences about inability.

My experiences as a school psychologist convinced me to return to the university and work on a multicultural Ph.D. at the University of New Mexico. My colleagues at UNM (a wonderfully diverse place) were surprised when I accepted a position at the University of North Dakota upon graduation. The University of North Dakota is very monocultural.

This seemed to me to be the perfect place to teach. The students were sound academically, had good work ethics, and a genuine desire to be the best teachers possible. What they generally lacked was an exposure to cultural and economic diversity, even though many of these monocultural students would teach in multicultural environments, often in the Southwest.

I took a sabbatical leave for one year and visited our graduates' classrooms in Texas, Arizona, and Nevada. It was apparent to me that although these young teachers did well, they would certainly benefit from more specific information about their Hispanic students. And so I participated in designing a class to better prepare preservice teachers for Hispanic students—a collaboration that introduced me to the reality that there was limited material available for this important area of study. This realization was the impetus for this book.

Toni Griego Jones, Ph.D.

I grew up wanting to be a teacher. I don't ever remember wanting to do or be anything else. When I started teaching in the Denver area in the late 1960s, I couldn't get enough of it. My first certification was in art education, but I taught in elementary classrooms most of my first years, and at various times taught art classes and English as a Second Language classes in the evenings, and religion classes on Sundays. When I spent a year in Latin America, I was also able to teach English to young children and to businessmen who were preparing to work in the United States.

Over the years, one of my greatest joys in teaching has been the great diversity of students I've been able to work with. I've taught in rural areas, in suburbs, and in the inner city when Denver was immersed in implementing the court's desegregation orders. Since I taught in bilingual and nonbilingual classrooms, my students were from the mainstream and from minority groups, including Vietnamese, Hmong, Laotians, Native Americans, African Americans, and Mexican Americans. I learned so much about so many different cultural groups, and particularly about my own, which is Mexican American. In my own schooling, there was relatively little taught about the history and contributions of Hispanics. Perhaps because I attended parochial schools, the curriculum did touch on contributions of Latin America and Spain to the Church so my schooling was not completely devoid of mention of Hispanics, but that aspect was extremely limited. This lack of attention to Hispanic heritage and presence in curriculum sparked a commitment to searching for content related to Hispanic populations in the United States. The need to provide useful and easily accessible information about Hispanic student populations was one of the reasons for writing this book.

As a balance to the joy I found in teaching, I also saw subtle, and sometimes not so subtle, discrimination against racial and ethnic minorities in schools. This discrimination relative to Hispanic students was often manifested by ignoring them, by not realizing their specific needs, or in attributing their problems to language barriers. This is another reason for writing this book: to call attention to this group of children who are often neglected in public schools.

After ten years as a teacher, I served as an administrator in the Denver Bilingual/ESL programs and for a short time in the Research and Development office. This administrative experience taught me the importance of addressing equity and students' rights at an institutional level and prompted a lifelong interest in studying how minority groups, specifically Hispanic populations, are involved in educational reforms so important to their children.

In 1988 I received my Ph.D. in social and multicultural foundations of education from the University of Colorado–Boulder and ventured off to the Midwest to take a position at the University of Wisconsin–Milwaukee in the Department of Curriculum and Instruction—this time to teach the teachers. One of my professorial responsibilities there was to develop teacher preparation programs for bilingual teachers and it was a tremendous growth experience for me. This was the first time I had contact with a variety of Hispanic groups—Puerto Ricans, Central Americans, South Americans, Dominicans, as well as Mexican Americans. As an educational consultant, I spent time on the Eastern seaboard, which further expanded my Hispanic horizons. I gained a respect for the diversity within Hispanic populations, but also learned to appreciate what we all have in common. Much of what I share in this book comes from insights gained from working with other Latino colleagues, students, and people in our communities.

Although I loved Wisconsin and the wonderful people there, I longed to be home in the Southwest and in 1996 took a position at the University of Arizona in the Department of Teaching and Teacher Education. In both universities, with the exception of many students in bilingual certification

Mary Lou Fuller and Toni Griego Jones

programs, most of my teacher education students were "the norm" for preservice teachers. That is, they were white, non-Hispanic, and female. In both universities, I found that teacher candidates cared deeply about children and wanted to be the best teachers for all children, but there was a general lack of awareness and understanding about cultural differences and how differences affect teaching and learning. I have worked at learning how to help my university students understand the diversity within K–12 schools and how they can make that diversity work for all, for teachers and children. This has sometimes been difficult work, and I hope this book will provide information and insight that will be useful to preservice teachers as well as to those teachers who are already in schools with Hispanic children.

CHAPTER 1 Hispanic Student Populations

Although I love being what I am, it is embarrassing to know what most people think of us.

—From an interview with Hispanic high school students in a midwestern city, mid-1990s

This chapter covers the following topics:

- The proliferation of "uncut diamonds" in the nation's schools, otherwise known as the change in Hispanic student demographics
- Importance of addressing the education of Hispanic students—to the nation as well as to students
- Overview of demographics
- The role of cultural background in schooling

Change in Hispanic Student Demographics

When I talked with the high schools students whose words are quoted above, their interviews were full of feelings of isolation, loneliness, and alienation from teachers and other students. They had very little interaction with students who were not Hispanic, expressed anxiety and confusion about how others perceived them, and felt they were being stereotyped as bad students. All students resented this stereotyping, but especially those who aspired to do well academically. These students were perfect examples of the uncut diamonds that the Hispanic parent in Arizona was describing.

This particular school had received an influx of Mexican American students in the early 1990s and was under a court order to improve programs for minority students, mostly African American, but increasingly Hispanic as well. I was deeply touched by the students' comments about their lives in school. They needed, even yearned for someone to listen to them, to pay attention to them. They wanted to like their teachers and administrators, but felt that the teachers and principals really didn't care about them. They existed on the margins, went to classes, but didn't really participate in school life. Adults rarely talked with them or showed that they knew or cared about what was happening to them. These Hispanic students were fluent in English and were not in bilingual programs, so there was no apparent reason for the lack of communication between teachers and students. However, when I talked with adults and asked them about their contact with students, they said that because they were not teachers in bilingual programs, they didn't have anything to do with these students. Teachers went through the day apparently not seeing the students who desperately needed to be recognized and valued. Students wanted to be part of the school, to do well in classes, and to participate in sports and extracurricular activities, but they felt invisible in this school where they were 5 percent of the student population. Teachers and administrators did not really know what to do with the students, they didn't completely understand the demographic changes taking place in their community and did not automatically accept responsibility for this "new" population of students.

The changes taking place in that midwestern town were not unique, nor were the reactions of students, teachers, and administrators. These changes were taking place throughout the country and school personnel needed to catch up with the demographics. This chapter provides an overview of information on Hispanic populations across the country and there are suggestions for more in-depth resources to study the origin of each major Hispanic group—Mexican American, Puerto Rican, Cuban, Central and South American, and other Caribbean countries.

Shift in Numbers and Location of Hispanic Students

AUTHOR'S NOTE **Toni Griego Jones**

The year I started teaching in an industrial suburb of Denver in the late 1960s, there were five new teachers in our school. I was the only native Coloradan and the only Hispanic. The other new teachers were from other states. In those days, most of the nation's teachers graduated from colleges and universities in the Midwest, and Denver area schools recruited heavily from out of state institutions. It was a surprise to me that the others did not already know about Hispanic children and thought of the few Hispanic students in our school as immigrants or newcomers. Apparently, they had not encountered Hispanic students before. The idea that teachers who had just moved to Colorado would think of Hispanics as foreigners surprised me because, aside from Native Americans, Hispanics were the first settlers of Colorado.

There were only two Hispanic children in my first elementary classroom in the late 1960s. Both were Mexican American; one child came from a family that had recently immigrated to the United States from Mexico and the other descended from the original settlers of Colorado with roots going back 350 years in what is now the United States. Years later, in the mid 1970s, I began teaching in the Denver inner city schools where about a third of the students were Hispanic, mostly Mexican American, clustered in the north, west, and downtown. Twenty years later, in the 1990s, Mexican American students made up over 50 percent of the student population in the Denver Public Schools. This demographic change occurred throughout the West and Southwest.

The only demographic information available about Hispanics in the 1960s was by region. The federal government did not collect data on Hispanic populations nationwide. The federal census in 1970 included a question on Hispanic origin, but was only asked of a 5 percent sample of households. Finally, information was collected on Hispanics for the first time on a national level in 1980 when Hispanics represented 6.4 percent of the population. By 1990, they accounted for 9 percent and by 2000, 12.5 percent. In the past, Hispanic children were enrolled primarily in large urban districts or in rural migrant schools. Percentages of Hispanics in suburban schools were relatively low. Changes in school demographics since that time have been dramatic. The Hispanic enrollment in rural districts has remained fairly stable, and although still largely in urban areas, Hispanic children are enrolled in all types of school districts. The largest numbers of Hispanic students are concentrated in California, Texas, New York, Florida, Illinois, Arizona, New Jersey, and New Mexico. They are now found in districts across the country—in urban, suburban, and rural districts.

Why Are These Demographics Important to Preservice Teachers and to Teacher Educators?

Unless schools do something dramatic, and soon, the country and Hispanics may lose their opportunity to create a new, dynamic, and prosperous future for everyone. The quickly growing Hispanic populations in schools offer a challenge, but they also offer great promise in terms of potential—talent, energy, and a desire to make better lives for themselves. According to economic reports, Hispanics are upwardly mobile when they get good educations. In a report by the Morrison Institute of Arizona State University, for example, the upward mobility of many Arizona Hispanics shows that the lack of preparation for higher paying jobs and further education can be overcome. Hispanics who are born in the United States especially, are making substantial gains in education and work. According to this report, by 1998 41 percent of households headed by U.S.-born Mexican Americans in Arizona were "middle class," as defined by annual income above $40,000, and Hispanics who attained comparable schooling to whites achieved comparable or superior economic outcomes (Morrison Institute for Public Policy, 2001, p. 20).

The problem for our society is that even though some Hispanic students are successful, *most* Hispanic students are not getting a good education, at least not a competitive education. They are not reaching the same levels of academic achievement as non-Hispanic Americans by any measure. Just as alarming, they are dropping out of school at higher levels. In some states, Hispanics will constitute over half the workforce. If they are only able to fill low-end service jobs, many of the open positions in higher-end jobs will go unfilled. Creating a permanent lower class made up primarily of one ethnic group can only lead to social unrest and economic decline. It is in the best interests of individual states and the country as a whole to educate its fastest growing minority group.

	Completed High School	**AA Degree**	**BA Degree**
Hispanic	25.9%	5.2%	10.3%
National	33.8%	7.3%	23.8%

Source: Tomás Rivera Policy Institute, 1998.

Better education in pre-K–12 schools for Hispanic students not only would have a positive effect in employment, but in increasing enrollment at colleges and universities. Not enough Hispanic students are entering colleges and universities. At the beginning of the new millenium, only 10 percent of Hispanic populations earned a Bachelor's degree or more compared to the national average of 24 percent (Tomás Rivera Policy Institute, 1998). Hispanics make up 12.5 percent of the total population, but in 1996–1997 they only received 3.7 percent of Master's degrees conferred, 2.4 percent of Doctorates, and 4.5 percent of professional degrees in the nation's universities ("The Nation," 2000).

Teachers and their relationships with Hispanic students are key to improving the education of Hispanic children. No amount of programs, curricular materials, or strategies can accomplish what a teacher who understands and cares about his/her students can. The important thing is that teachers know they need to develop an understanding of the sociocultural and economic contexts of all their students. The social and economic consequences of neglecting the education of Hispanic students are serious and negative for American society as well as for individual Hispanic students. But, the payoff for proactively addressing the education of this growing segment of the population will be positive and energizing for American society. We believe that casting the education of Hispanic students in terms of advantages to our country, as well as individuals, will be more doable than to continue thinking of Hispanic students as "problems" to be solved. The negative, deficit framework of defining Hispanic children as problems has not worked. To think of the education of Hispanics as a revitalization of American education is certainly a more energizing way to approach this challenge.

Overview of Hispanic Demographics

Definition of Terms

The term *Hispanic* is an umbrella term that is primarily sociopolitical used to describe all groups of people whose national and/or cultural origins include the Spanish language and heritage. The major national origin subgroups that are under the Hispanic umbrella are Mexican American, Puerto Rican, Cuban, Central and South American, Caribbean, and Dominican Republic. The Hispanic umbrella includes people born in the United States and immigrants to this country.

Many people of Hispanic origin prefer the term *Latino*, perhaps because it is identified more with Latin America. This term seems to be used more in the midwest and east coast, while *Hispanic* is often used in the West and Southwest and is used in the federal census taken every ten years. Both Latino and Hispanic are used in educational literature, but in fact, most people generally call *themselves* by their more specific national origin name, that is, Mexican American, Cuban American, Puerto Rican, and so forth. The important thing for teachers is that whatever term they use needs to be used with respect.

Within Hispanic national origin subgroups, there are even more specific terms. For example, there are several names used for Mexican Americans, such as Chicano and Mejicano. The term *Chicano* is a term adopted by young political activists in the 50s and 60s and refers to people of Mexican descent born in the United States. Some older generations react negatively to being called Chicano because they associate the name with activist, radical activity. People who were born in Mexico and were naturalized citizens prefer to be called Mexican. The best thing for preservice and inservice teachers to do is to find out from the local community what they would like to be called. Many will answer that it doesn't matter as long as it is used respectfully. Any term is not acceptable if used in a derogatory way.

Diversity within the Hispanic Population

Hispanics can be of any race and may include white, black, and people of mixed races. They are generally identified according to national origin. In looking at the demographics for Hispanic students, it is helpful to look at overall figures. The Hispanic population is the fastest growing ethnic/cultural group in the United States and the largest of the non-European populations. In 2000 the Hispanic population surpassed the African Americans as the largest minority group in the United States. Hispanics in the United States presently represent 12 percent (representing 32.8 million people) of the total population. Because *Hispanic* is an umbrella term, representing people whose history and original language have been influenced by Spain as well as indigenous Indian cultures, it is important to look and see who is under the umbrella (Figure 1.1). Mexican Americans represent the largest group (58.5 percent). Others in order of population are Puerto Ricans (9 percent), Central and South Americans (8.6 percent), Cubans (4 percent), and "other" (17.3 percent) (U.S. Census, 2000). At the end of the chapter there are resources for more in-depth reading on each of the major population groups. The following are quick overviews of each group.

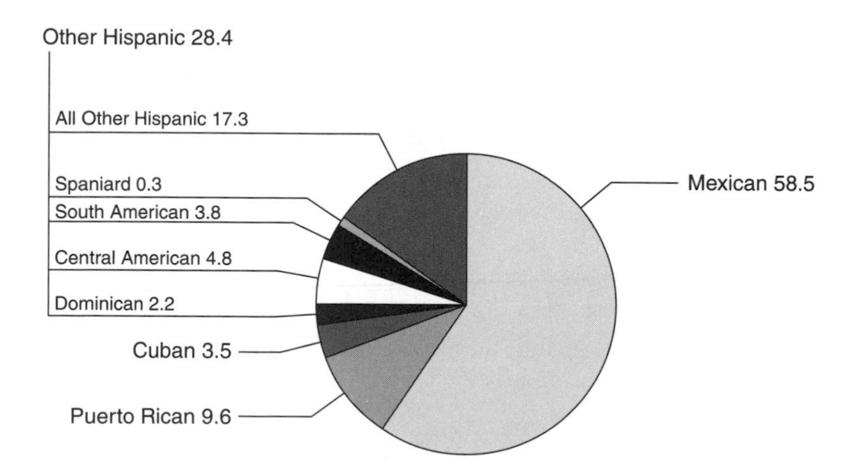

FIGURE 1.1 Diversity within the Hispanic Population
Source: U.S. Census Bureau, Census 2000 Summary File 1.

Mexican Americans. The Mexican American population resides primarily in the West and Southwest. Half of all Hispanics live in just two states, California (31 percent) and Texas (19 percent), and the majority of these Hispanics are Mexican American. The majority of Hispanics in Arizona, Colorado, New Mexico, and all the western states are also Mexican American. Forty-two percent of the population in New Mexico is Mexican American. Many are immigrants who have recently come to the United States, but the majority are second, third, and even beyond, generation and have deep roots in the Southwest. Even though most Mexican Americans live in the West, they are widely distributed in the United States with populations in all states, including Hawaii and Alaska. Illinois has one of the largest Mexican American populations with more than a million concentrated near Chicago. Mexican Americans have one of the widest range of socioeconomic levels with a substantial middle class in the largest states, even though many work as laborers and in blue collar jobs.

The demographic distribution of Mexican Americans is spreading. States like Minnesota have a growing population of Mexican residents and they aren't just in the large urban areas. Crookston and Moorhead, Minnesota are good examples of this phenomenon. Dalton, Georgia (population 27,000) has three Spanish language newspapers. And as one non-Hispanic resident of Dalton observed, "We're a border community—1,000 miles away from the border" (Gibbs, 2001, p. 39).

Puerto Ricans. Puerto Rico is part of the United States, so all Puerto Ricans are U. S. citizens, not "immigrants." They travel freely between the island and the mainland, and nearly as many Puerto Ricans live in the 50 states as live in Puerto Rico. The 3.4 million maintain a strong identity as Puerto Ricans and have had a significant influence on the East Coast where they are the predominant Spanish-speaking group in large cities like New York. The colonial relationship between the United States and Puerto Rico has affected Puerto Rican culture and language and sometimes causes dissension about governance, yet pride in being Puerto Rican is strong, generation after generation. The Midwest also has increasing numbers of Puerto Rican students.

Cubans. Cubans are different from other Hispanic populations in that they came to the United States as political exiles in the early 1960s, not as immigrants who intended to settle permanently in the United States. They are the only Hispanic population whose large scale immigration was initially subsidized by the United States government with special privileges accorded by the United States. Those who left Cuba after the revolution in 1959 had had close ties with the United States for many years and sought refuge in this country when their government was overthrown. Initially, they came for political reasons, but more recently emigrants are coming for economic and personal reasons as well. The original emigrants were committed to overthrowing the current Cuban government and returning to Cuba, but the younger generation of Cuban Americans seems to be grounded in the United States. Many who came in the 1960s were professional and business people and settled in Florida where more than half of the 1.2 million still live.

Central and South Americans. Central Americans represent 4.8 percent of the total Hispanic population, with 655,000 Salvadorans, 372,000 Guatemalans and 281,000 Hondurans accounting for most of them. South Americans (3.8 percent of total Hispanic population) come mostly from Colombia, Ecuador, and Peru. The relative percentage of Central and South Americans is increasing even though their numbers are not as large as those of Mexican American, Puerto Rican, and Cuban populations. They come for a variety of reasons, ranging from political unrest to the need for better jobs and are spread across the country.

Other Hispanics. The "other" category includes people from the Caribbean islands, from Spain, and other Spanish speaking territories or countries. One significant group that is growing in numbers along the Eastern seaboard is Dominicans. They are replacing Puerto Ricans in traditional barrios in cities like New York where Dominicans have been the leading source of legal immigrants for the last three decades of the twentieth century. Many came to escape political unrest, but also to look for jobs or set up small businesses in large cities (Sunshine & Warner, 1998).

Age of Population

Hispanic populations are younger and growing faster than the mainstream population. Thirty-five percent of the population is less than 18 years old, while 23.5 percent of the mainstream population fall in this category. Also only 5.3 percent of the Hispanic population is 65 years or older while 14 percent of the mainstream population is past that age (Therrien & Rameriz, 2001). Figure 1.2 compares ages among different Hispanic groups.

Employment

Hispanics are more likely to work in service related jobs (19.4 percent) as opposed to their Anglo counterparts (see Figure 1.3). While conversely, only 14 percent of Hispanics are in managerial or professional positions (compared to 32.2 percent among non-Hispanics). Considering the nature of their employment opportunities, Hispanics also make significantly less than the white non-Hispanic population. Although 27.4 percent of non-Hispanic whites make $50,000 or more only 9.6% of the Hispanic population do (Therrien & Rameriz, 2001).

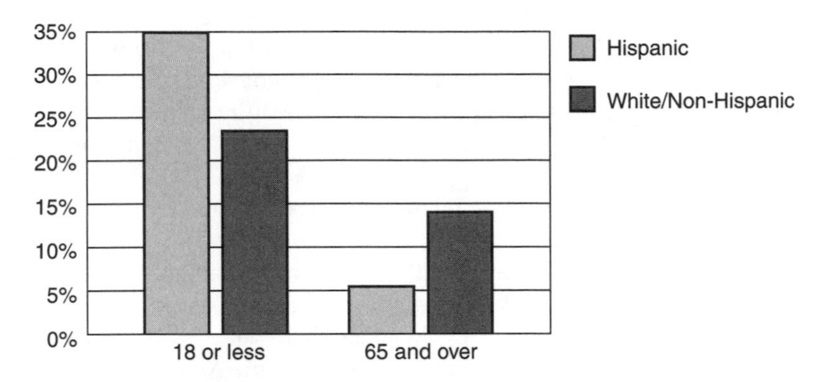

FIGURE 1.2 Age of Population

Source: U.S. Census Bureau, Census 2000 Summary File 1.

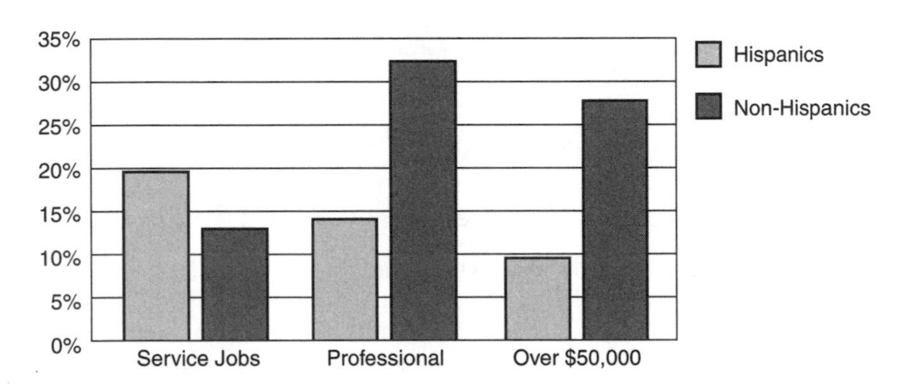

FIGURE 1.3 Employment Data for Hispanics

Source: Therrien & Ramirez, 2001.

The Role of Culture in Schooling

What Is Culture?

With all the focus on awareness of the culture of minority groups, it may be easy for white students to conclude that they have no culture. In fact though everyone has a culture. Culture can be defined as the sum total of beliefs, attitudes, and behaviors that any given group holds. There are three things we need to remember about culture. First, it is learned. Every child is born into a particular cultural group and learns its ways. It is not something we inherit in our genes. For example, a Japanese child who is born in the United States learns the American culture, not Japanese. The second thing to remember is that it is shared. All members of any cultural group share the beliefs, values, attitudes, and patterns of behaviors of the group, even though individuals have their own personality differences within the group. Finally, the third point to remember is that culture is dynamic and is always changing. Groups come into contact with each other and they influence each other. The minute that students enter a school and come in contact with children and teachers from different cultural backgrounds, they begin to influence each other. For example, Nicaraguan immigrant students living within the United States are not "experiencing" the exact same culture as Nicaraguan students in Nicaragua. They may share same historical roots, but their current experiences are greatly influenced by the American context they live in. It is important for prospective teachers to remember that American culture is made up of the cultural patterns of behavior of all its inhabitants, minorities as well as European American.

In today's world, culture is greatly influenced by contact through the electronic media as well as by physical contact. Within the United States, the media plays a powerful role in "homogenizing" American culture. In spite of regional differences, people across America receive the same messages through the media. Through the media, American culture also influences people in other countries via American movies, music, and art.

Cultural Connections between Teachers and Students

The reason we have to learn about culture is that it determines how people understand the world and what they do. Children are socialized by their cultural group to value particular things and to behave in certain ways. When the children's ways are similar to those of the teacher, they are more likely to understand each others expectations. For example, children learn how to interact and talk with adults, they learn when it is appropriate to talk, when it is their turn to say something, who they should talk to, and what they should talk about. When teachers and children come from different cultural groups, there is a good chance that they may have misunderstandings about everyday things they each take for granted.

AUTHOR'S NOTE Toni Griego Jones

Although I have lectured many times on culture and how it shapes perspectives, a preservice teacher reminded me just how ingrained the role of culture is in how teachers learn about "other children" and teaching. This preservice teacher asked a question that acutely sharpened my class' awareness of what the term "cultural perspective" means. One day a Native American guest speaker came to our educational foundations class and told us about the history of the American government's attempts to eradicate Native American culture and identity by sending Indian children to boarding schools. After his informative talk, a student who fit the profile of most preservice teachers, White middle class female, asked him if Indian students had to pay tuition for the opportunity to attend boarding school or was it free for American Indians. My first reaction was that the question was disrespectful and smart-alecky, but I knew this student to be a conscientious student who always had questions about the class lectures or readings. The speaker looked surprised and I suspect he didn't know what motivated such a question. Suddenly, I realized that this student, who was from the East Coast, thought that boarding schools were a privilege enjoyed only by wealthy, privileged families. She thought of boarding schools as prestigious schools, as something only well-connected, wealthy families could afford. What the speaker was saying about the painful, even cruel experience of forcing Indian children to leave home and lose their cultural identity didn't click with the student because her image of "boarding school" was so set. Attending boarding schools was, from her perspective, a positive, privileged experience. The term "boarding school" had such totally opposite images for each of the people in that question and answer exchange (preservice student and guest speaker) that she completely misunderstood most of what he talked about. I think she understood that Indian children had been unhappy in their boarding schools, but she still really didn't *understand* because she perceived boarding schools as something privileged and something only few people get.

Students in pre-K–12 schools come from many different cultural groups, especially in large urban districts, so it may seem impossible for teachers to learn about the cultures of all different groups. But, if teachers recognize that there are differences and that those differences are important to understand in order to teach effectively, they are more likely to be effective teachers, that is, the children in their classrooms are more likely to learn. Preservice teachers sometimes worry that they cannot learn about every cultural group that is represented in school systems. That is probably true, but it is important to learn about the cultural backgrounds of the children in their own classrooms. However, even though it is not always possible to learn about every cultural group, indeed, it may not be possible to learn about each Hispanic national origin group, it is possible for teachers to:

- Be aware that there are differences in the way cultural groups understand things
- Accept and respect differences and not be judgemental about them
- Learn as much as they can about the cultural backgrounds of children in their classrooms

Sometimes my preservice teachers have argued that it does more harm than good to focus on differences. They say it makes things worse when preservice teachers are "forced" to learn about other people's cultures. They also worry that acknowledging differences promotes those differences and causes disunity within our society. American history argues against this position. For most of our history, educators have ignored cultural differences, but they didn't go away. At some point in their careers, they will have to face diversity within their classroom. They can make it work for the good of all, or they can perpetuate the failure of a substantial number of students in their care.

Professional Reflection

The following are excerpts from preservice teachers' writings. The writings range from negative to positive on the question of whether to have a "multicultural requirement" for education majors. Read the excerpts and decide where you fit in the continuum. Write your own opinion about requiring multicultural study as part of teacher preparation. How do you think you formed this opinion?

1. "I think the students shouldn't have to take a whole class on the issue. This should be a unit plan that is maybe 3 weeks. There are more important things for students to learn such as math. It really seems like a waste of time."
2. "I think I am a fence rider. It would be great for students to learn about each other's culture, especially if there is racial tension. On the other hand, there are so many different cultures, how could we make sure they are *all* addressed?"
3. "Exposing students to other cultures not only educates them, it helps all students feel that they are members of the learning community/environment in the classroom. The more we as teachers accumulate knowledge regarding different groups, the more our students will feel included."

Teachers' Responsibility toward Hispanic Students

Context for Responsibility. Teachers are accountable for teaching all children, but the context for teaching Hispanic students can't be described in the same way. It is too different from one part of the country to another. Even schooling for one national origin group is not the same, depending on geographic region. For example, Mexican American students are enrolled in districts across the country but the teaching contexts for all Mexican American children are not the same across the country. There are classrooms in Texas, California, and New Mexico that are 100 percent Mexican American while other classrooms in Wisconsin, South Carolina, and Idaho have only a few. The only unifying theme may be the alienation students sometimes feel and the resulting academic underachievement and drop out rates.

In some cities such as San Antonio, where Hispanic parents constitute a significant percentage of voters, the political clout of Hispanic communities regarding school board policies, resources and so forth, makes a difference in resources, materials, personnel. In these cases, there is evidence that the total involvement of the community in their own schools makes a difference in academic achievement for Hispanic children. But, what happens to those who are lost in schools where they are a minority, especially where they feel ignored, even shunned? In classrooms where the majority of students are Hispanic of whatever national origin, what is the teachers' job? Will it be different from the teacher who has only one or two Hispanic children in the classroom?

Personal Relationships. In interviewing Mexican American students over the years in the Midwest and in the Southwest, there were some common themes that emerged from interviews. Hispanic students often feel that no one cares for them, that no one expects much from them, that they are outsiders, and they don't belong. Even though Hispanic children generally feel valued and nurtured by their own families and local communities, they feel that the larger society, including our educational institutions, does not care and value them. It is this atmosphere that each teacher can change in schools. The climate and teachers' caring have a great effect on what *happens to* Hispanic students in classrooms as well as what students *do* in classrooms.

There is sufficient research and practical experience to guide educators in knowing what factors contribute to effective schooling for Hispanic students. In most cases, these factors are important in teaching all children, but seem to be absolutely critical in teaching Hispanic children. For example, research on effective schools for Hispanic students points out that personal interaction with teachers, nurturing from teachers, is a critical component for Mexican American students. Without this, the alienation many of them feel toward public schools and toward a society that "puts them down" overtakes them and they are at high risk for dropping out (Garcia, 2000).

A more nurturing type of teaching may enhance learning for most American students, but it is absolutely critical to the success of most Mexican American students. The impersonal, competitive environments of many schools, particularly secondary schools, appear to be fostering alienation, anger, even violence, or, if not fostering, certainly not providing the emotional support many children need to survive. If we think about it, the students at Columbine High School generally had high academic achievement scores so everyone thought the school was doing a good job. Yet, would a focus on the emotional health of children have helped those students?

Parents as Partners. Another key factor in successfully working with Hispanic students is the absolute necessity of connecting with parents and community. This focus, too, could be of tremendous value in educating all students. How to effectively work with parents is something that prospective educators receive little or no preparation for. Although there is widespread consensus that parent involvement is important and facilitates teaching, there is little real commitment to making this a part of teacher education. Perhaps the tremendous importance that Hispanic populations put on family will be one of the Hispanic communities greatest contributions to American public education. Many of the research findings on effective practices in teaching Hispanic children are, in fact, good for everybody.

Bottom Line. By the year 2000 Hispanics became the largest minority population in the United States—12.4 percent of the total population. Some who worry about this statistic can spend time fighting this reality and holding on to the past, just as many tried to do with previous demographic shifts in our country. Those who believe in people and the democratic principles of the United States can begin to adjust and make schooling work for all our citizens.

In the end, it is the teacher's responsibility to maximize the learning for all students whether they constitute the majority of the class or a small minority. Hispanics are the most segregated student population with a third of Hispanic students attending schools that are predominantly Hispanic, but there are still many classrooms where they are part of an ethnic and cultural mix. Teachers in predominantly Hispanic schools may only have that cultural group to learn about. But for the teachers who have a mix, it is important that they do not see their job as split—doing some things for Hispanics and doing other things for other ethnic groups. Their teaching can change to include all, to integrate all cultural backgrounds to enhance learning for all children.

EXERCISES FOR REFLECTION

1. **Everyone has a culture; what is mine?** How would you describe the culture of the town or city where you grew up? How do you think it differs from other towns or cities? How is your culture influenced by your ethnic/racial background?

2. **How to describe American culture.** How would you describe American culture? What are its characteristics? What do Americans value? Believe?

How do they act? What makes Americans different from everyone else? Have you ever been in a foreign country? Have you been able to "spot" another American? How?

3. **How to learn about other cultural groups.** Sometimes students feel that learning about other cultural groups is an impossible task, too overwhelming to contemplate, and so they often like to avoid it. Many teacher preparation programs do not always incorporate learning about cultural groups different from our own into courses, field experiences, or readings. At most, programs will have a course on multicultural education. The following suggestions are ideas taken from colleges and universities that have tried various ways of helping preservice teachers learn more about other cultural groups in meaningful, relevant, and belief changing ways.

4. **Learn from the community.** One of the most effective ways of learning about people who live in a community different from our own is to visit that community. Using the same idea behind studying abroad in a foreign country, preservice teachers can learn about new neighborhoods and communities by visiting them. The important thing is to keep an open mind and to have a respectful and non-judgmental attitude. Look for experiences that allow you to explore various aspects of students' lives—economic, social, educational, political, and cultural. Even though a visit is a limited experience, it can serve to introduce preservice and practicing teachers to the communities served by schools. Find a friend or teacher who does know the community to get an idea of what and where to visit. Then, after the experience, debrief or share experiences with that person, ask questions to clarify or explain what you experienced. If you don't know anyone, a good place to start is often a community center that is open to the public. Community centers often have bulletin boards with information about things going on in the community so you can learn a lot about what is important in the community, who is active in the community, what resources are in the community, and about their needs. Other "learning places" are restaurants, museums, department stores, grocery stores, churches, and libraries. Some teacher educators have called visits to other communities "community plunges," culture walks, cultural scavenger hunts, field trips, and cultural immersions. Write down questions, observations, and comments to reflect on and learn more about.

   For more about immersing yourself in multicultural experiences, see: "Strategies for Preparing Culturally Responsive Teachers" by A. G. Leavell, M. Cowart, and R. W. Wilhelm in *Equity & Excellence in Education*, Vol. 32, No. 1; and *Beyond Heroes and Holidays: A Practical Guide to K–12 Anti-Racist, Multicultural Education and Staff Development*, edited by Enid Lee, Deborah Menkart, Margo Okazawa-Rey. Available from the Center for Language Minority Education and Research (CLMER) at NECA, P.O. Box 73038, Washington, DC 20056-3038, 800-763-9131, fax: 202-238-0109, e-mail: necadc@aol.com.

5. **Learn through readings.** As prospective and practicing teachers, we are lifelong learners and one of our most effective methods of learning is to

read.There are many fine sources of information about each Hispanic subgroup available at libraries and bookstores. There is a good listing in the last chapter on resources or see below for our favorites. However, it is important not to just read *about* Hispanic populations; it is important to read what they themselves have written. By reading what Hispanic authors from all groups have written, we can begin to understand what they value, believe, and how they live. We can begin to see similarities between cultures as well as how we differ. Reading "multicultural" literature is sometimes a more comfortable way to learn about other cultures than immersing ourselves in experiences with others, but reading does need to be followed up with real life experience.

RESOURCES FOR HISPANIC POPULATIONS

Mexican Americans

The Missions of New Mexico, 1776 by Fray Francisco Atanasio Dominguez, Translated and annotated by Eleanor B. Adams and Fray Angelico Chavez. Available from The University of New Mexico Press.

Mexican-Origin People in the United States, A Topical History. By Oscar J. Martinez, available from The University of Arizona Press in Tucson. ISBN: 0-8165-1179-9, ISBN: 0-8165-2089-5 (pbk)

Puerto Ricans

Puerto Ricans, Born in the U.S.A. by Clara E. Rodriguez published by Unwin Hyman, Inc. in Boston. ISBN: 0-04-497041-2, ISBN: 0-04-497042-0 (pbk).

Caribbean Connections, Moving North Edited by Catherine A. Sunshine and Keith O. Warner. Contact: Network of Educators on the Americas, PO Box 73038, Washington, DC 20056 or call 202-238-2379 or 202-429-0137. Email: necadc@aol.com, ISBN: 1-878554-12-3

Cubans

Caribbean Connections, Moving North. Edited by Catherine A. Sunshine and Keith O. Warner. Contact: Network of Educators on the Americas, P.O. Box 73038, Washington, DC 20056 or call 202-238-2379, 202-429-0137. Email: necadc@aol.com, ISBN: 1-878554-12-3

All Populations

Latinos Unidos, from Cultural Diversity to the Politics of Solidarity (1999) by Henry Trueba, New York: Rowman & Littlefield Publishers, Inc.

Beck, S. A. L., & Allexsaht-Snider, M. (2002). Recent language minority education policy in Georgia: Appropriation, assimilation, and Americanization. In S. Wortham, E. G. Murrillo, & E. T. Hamann (Eds.), *Education in the New Latino Disaspora: Policy and the Politics of Identity* (pp. 37–66). Westport, CT: Ablex.

REFERENCES

Garcia, E. E. (2000). *Hispanic education.* Lanham, MD: Rowman & Littlefield Publishers, Inc.

Gibbs, N. (2001, June 11). Welcome to America. *Time 157*(23), 39.

Guzman, B. (2001, May). *The Hispanic Population, Census 2000 Brief.* Washington: U.S. Department of Commerce.

Morrison Institute for Public Policy. (2001). *Five shoes waiting to drop.* Tempe: Arizona State University, p. 20.

The nation, students. (2000, September 1). *The Chronicle of Higher Education Almanac Issue*, p. 32.

Therrien, M., & Ramirez, R. R. (2001). *The Hispanic population in the United States.* Washington: U.S. Department of Commerce.

Thomás Rivera Policy Institute. (1998). Claremont, CA: Author. www.trpi.org.

CHAPTER

2 Reflecting on Our Own Beliefs about Hispanic Students

One's personal predispositions are not only relevant but, in fact, stand at the core of becoming a teacher.
—Dan Lortie, *Schoolteacher: A Sociological Study*

This chapter covers the following topics:

- Research on the role of teacher beliefs and why it is important to assess preservice and inservice teachers' beliefs
- Beliefs as the focus of change in teacher preparation
- Literature on beliefs and knowledge of preservice and inservice teachers regarding racial/ethnic and linguistic minorities
- Literature on beliefs and knowledge of preservice teachers and inservice teachers regarding Hispanic populations

This chapter is about the importance of understanding ourselves as products of a cultural group and how each of us develops beliefs and understandings of our own cultural group as well as others. It begins with a discussion about beliefs and the important role they play in learning to teach. At the end of the chapter, the readers will be given exercises designed to elicit personal reflections on their beliefs, attitudes, and knowledge about Hispanic populations.

How Beliefs Affect Preservice Teachers' Learning

When students decide to enter teacher preparation programs, they bring a lifetime's worth of experiences with them. Those experiences have led them to believe certain things about schools, about how children learn, and about what teaching means. Beliefs affect how preservice teachers learn about teaching in two ways. First, they strongly influence *what* and *how* prospective teachers learn. The existing beliefs preservice teachers bring with them determine what they build on, what they accept or reject from their teacher preparation programs. For example, if preservice teachers believe that Hispanic children do not value education, it will be difficult for preservice teachers to have high expectations for Hispanic students. Current constructivist theories that view learning as an active, constructive process acknowledge that existing knowledge and beliefs strongly influence individuals as they approach a learning task (Fang, 1996; Nespor, 1987; Pajares, 1992).

Second, beliefs are the pivot that has to change in order for teachers to learn new ways (Richardson, 1996). If preservice teachers' beliefs bind them in their ways of thinking about schools, about what good teaching is, or about children from backgrounds like their own or different from their own, they will not be open to learning about new ways to approach teaching or to relating to people from other cultural backgrounds. Preservice teachers encounter new ideas, theories, and ways of thinking about teaching when they take courses in teacher education. Some of these new ideas and theories will resonate with preservice teachers, others will go against their currently held beliefs. For example, the idea of taking cultural backgrounds into account in teaching may be new for preservice teachers. If they don't believe that cultural backgrounds are important to understand in teaching, they won't accept any of the theory or practice related to the role of culture in teaching. The beliefs need to be understood and addressed before teaching information about culture and culturally relevant methodologies and activities.

Where Do Beliefs Come From?

Preservice teachers' beliefs come from their own experiences as students in elementary and secondary schools, from their personal experiences with family, friends, and society, and to some extent from their teacher preparation programs. Research indicates that the most powerful influence on teacher candidates' beliefs comes from the first of these, from their own experiences in schools. Prospective teachers learned what teaching means by watching and interacting with their own teachers for at least twelve years prior to going to college. They learned to define and value education and all aspects of schooling from their parents and from their immediate circle of friends. Parents and family also transmit beliefs about other people and groups of people, those who are like themselves and those who are different. The larger society also influences what preservice teachers believe about other people, particularly through the media. In other words, contacts and interactions with others in homes, schools, and the larger society determine our beliefs and understandings of ourselves and others.

When it comes to the area of teaching culturally and linguistically diverse students, research indicates that the majority of preservice teachers have had very little contact with the diversity of students prior to entering teacher education programs (Zimpher & Ashburn, 1992). They have not experienced cultures and languages other than their own, and this has resulted in lack of knowledge and in parochial beliefs about minority children. Gomez and Tabachnick (1992) even suggest that views of prospective teachers could actually limit minority children's opportunities to benefit from schooling because of the parochialism inherent in the beliefs of those going into teaching. If preservice teachers never had experiences with Hispanic or other ethnic and language minority children, they don't have much to draw on when trying to learn how to teach *all* children in the cultural mix in schools.

Everyone is socialized within his/her own cultural group and each person develops beliefs about others primarily from their own families, neighbors, school mates, and from the larger society. Today the popular media also plays an enormous role in influencing the public's perceptions of racial and ethnic minorities. It is only human to understand the world from our own personal background experiences. Everyone does. However, the *professional* demand on teachers is that they learn enough about the role of culture in determining children's behaviors *and* the role of culture in determining their own behaviors relative to teaching children from a variety of cultural backgrounds. Because teaching is basically a matter of relationships with many different people (i.e., students) in the classroom setting, the teacher is required to relate to a great diversity of people at any given time. This includes diversity of special learning needs and economic backgrounds as well as racial and ethnic backgrounds. When the students and teacher are from the same cultural background there is generally some intuitive, unspoken understanding about societal norms. Teachers make assumptions about the values, beliefs, and resulting behaviors that will be mostly accurate, given that all the classroom participants come from the same background experience. When there are different cultural and socioeconomic differences, the *almost* automatic understanding of common beliefs and behaviors isn't there. This does not mean, however, that preservice and inservice teachers cannot learn about other cultural groups.

Beliefs as the Focus of Change in Teacher Education

Because of their importance in how preservice teachers learn, beliefs should be a focus in teacher preparation and in the ongoing development of teachers. Knowledge about pedagogy and subject matter are not the only things that are important for prospective teachers. The point of this chapter is to help prospective teachers and those already in teaching to reflect on how they perceive Hispanic children and to consciously develop beliefs that will guide their behaviors in teaching Hispanic children effectively. This type of self-reflection will in fact help in teaching all children, but particularly those who come from backgrounds different from those of preservice and inservice teachers.

Developing teacher behaviors that help teach children of diverse cultural backgrounds won't happen unless there is a conscious effort to examine our own beliefs and modify them if necessary—even more knowledge about methodologies won't result in more effective teaching without a change in core beliefs about people and about differences. Figure 2.1 lists common stereotypes about Hispanics in U.S. society.

AUTHOR'S NOTE Toni Griego Jones

In order to understand what society believes about Hispanic and other minority groups, I ask students in my educational foundations courses about stereotypes about major racial/ethnic groups in the United States. The lists are generated anonymously, but we discuss them in class and students are generally forthright about where the stereotypes come from. Students believe that there is some core of truth that gives rise to the stereotype, good or bad, but they generally do not have personal experience to verify or discount any of them. The stereotypes that surface most about Hispanics are that they are poor, lazy, uneducated, and hard working. Students see that stereotypes can be negative or positive, but that they are overgeneralizations about a group of people. Without concrete knowledge and some understanding of a cultural group, stereotypes can't help but influence the beliefs preservice teachers hold about any given group.

FIGURE 2.1 Stereotypes about Hispanic Populations

The following are 10 most frequently listed "stereotypes" by preservice teachers in author's educational foundations classes, in order of greatest frequency.

1. Poor
2. Lazy
3. Uneducated
4. Hard working
5. Manual laborers
6. Illegal immigrants
   Stupid
7. Family oriented
   Involved with gangs
8. Beautiful artists
   Drunks
   Trouble makers
   Moochers
   Religious
9. Drug dealers
   Dirty
10. Irresponsible
    Hot tempered
    Low riders
    Rude
    Excelling in society
    High drop outs
    Anti-conformists
    Overweight
    Dark skinned

Sometimes teachers only want tips on what to do or not do so as not to offend children from different cultural backgrounds. They want some quick magic activities that will appeal to "cultural values" or somehow tap into the cultural heritage of minority children. But, this is not enough. Preservice teachers have to understand ethnic and racial minority children, including Hispanic children as people, as members of a particular cultural group, *and* as part of American society—a society that is defined by all its inhabitants, not just by Anglo or northern European Americans. When they understand children as products of a cultural group, when they understand the values, beliefs, and behaviors of a given cultural group, then teachers can develop strategies and activities that are relevant and culturally sensitive. If they do not understand what is important to any given cultural group, no amount of methods and activities will help teachers connect to their Hispanic students.

Because of the importance of beliefs in learning how to teach, especially in learning how to teach culturally and linguistically different students, each chapter in this book will keep reminding the reader to examine his/her own beliefs about teaching and about Hispanic children. The body of research showing the effectiveness of identifying and modifying preservice teachers' beliefs, including beliefs about minority children, as part of teacher preparation programs is growing (Cabello & Davis-Burstein, 1995; Pajares, 1992). Given that schools are still failing in their efforts to educate Hispanic children, researching beliefs held by preservice teachers is a promising and urgent area to promote in teacher preparation.

What We Know about Teachers' Beliefs about Racial, Ethnic, and Linguistic Minorities

History

Teachers in general have not had a great deal of experience with cultural groups other than their own, even when they live close by or in the same city. This is true of all teachers regardless of their racial/ethnic backgrounds. Most teachers, preservice and inservice, come from white, middle class backgrounds and their knowledge and understanding of students who come from non-white or lower economic backgrounds tends to be understandably limited. White preservice teachers are not alone in their limited understanding of other cultural groups, however. Racial and ethnic minorities who go into teaching also come from backgrounds where they have had relatively little contact with other cultural groups. Minorities who become teachers also tend to be from middle class economic backgrounds. The only difference is that, because minorities usually have had to learn about the majority culture and how to live in it, they are more likely to be bicultural, that is, to be able to function in two cultures or societies.

Inservice Teachers

Because many teachers don't have opportunities to learn about cultural groups other than their own in teacher preparation programs, school districts have tried to teach teachers about other groups through staff development within districts. This type of staff development started after the Civil Rights movement of the 1960s when there was a rush to include "multicultural content" into curriculum and teaching methodologies. Publishing companies put out "multicultural" books and materials and school districts adopted them without much thought to how teachers, preservice and inservice, felt about the new "culturally sensitive" pedagogy. School districts adopted curriculum and held inservices to instruct teachers how to teach various racial/ethnic populations, but they totally underestimated the task of reorienting faculty to teach to diversity. No one took the time to investigate what teachers already knew or more importantly, what they *believed* about the various racial and ethnic groups they were now supposed to be attending to.

AUTHOR'S NOTE Toni Griego Jones

I remember once giving a mandated inservice on a Saturday morning to a group of teachers in Wisconsin. They were required to take a certain number of "human relations" credits for their recertification and they apparently had to attend at least one inservice on each of the major racial/ethnic minority groups. Being one of a few Hispanic faculty members at the University, I was often asked to give "the talk" on Hispanic populations—everything you always wanted to know, but never thought to ask, in one 3-hour session. This time, we were well into the Saturday morning session, which included information on Hispanic demographics, history, educational issues, and so forth, when a teacher at the back of the room, a white male, raised his hand and said what he wanted to know was why Hispanics wanted their share in schools and society but didn't want to contribute in things like military duty and fighting in our wars. He believed that Hispanics did not join the military forces and that they had not participated in any of our military conflicts.

In fact, Hispanics are overrepresented in the military forces, particularly in the fighting units, and had one of the highest percentage of casualties in the Vietnam War, the Korean War, and World War II relative to the general population. They also have one of the highest percentages of Medal of Honor recipients relative to their numbers in the military. All in the audience were surprised by the information I gave them about Hispanic participation in the military forces, including history about New Mexican regiments that fought for the Union in the Civil War and the financial aid Spain had given to the American Revolution.

This teacher complained about having to spend his time attending these sessions (although they were paid) and kept interrupting my talk until he was booed and told to be quiet by the teachers. The point of the story is this: No amount of knowledge was going to change that teacher's teaching because he firmly believed that Hispanics did not "deserve" to be understood and given special attention. His *beliefs* needed to change before the staff development inservice could do any good.

Research on Beliefs/Attitudes about Cultural Diversity

In the wake of frustration over mandated inservice training about racial and ethnic minorities and the limited success of preparing teachers for teaching a diverse student population, more studies addressing teachers' attitudes and beliefs toward racial and ethnic minorities began to appear in the late 1980s and 1990s. Some of these studies specifically addressed preservice teachers' beliefs about teaching minority children and indicated that preservice teachers who are typically white (but not exclusively) and lower to middle class believe that teaching children from different cultural groups is problematic and they are apprehensive about teaching them (Gomez, 1994; Groulx, 2001; Montecinos & Rios, 1999). By the end of the 20th century there was much more research and scholarly work available that documents the importance of addressing the cognitive, affective, and attitudinal perspectives of teachers and prospective teachers. Authors like Sonia Nieto, Geneva Gay, James Banks, Carl Grant, Christine Sleeter, Lisa Delpit, Carlos Cortes, and Louise Derman-Sparks among many others, write about how teacher expectations, racism, cultural parochialism, and privilege can influence teachers in their interactions with racial/ethnic groups different than their own. Some authors (Gary Howard, Vivian Paley) specifically address how white teachers need to reflect on their own beliefs and dispositions held from positions of privilege in American society. Preservice teachers who go into teaching believing that they love *all* children and can make a difference in their lives, find that they are unprepared for the challenges of dealing with children who come from backgrounds different than the ones they are used to. Many begin to perceive the children as problems, never thinking that part of the problem may lie within themselves, in their own lack of understanding the children. The responsibility for the lack of understanding lies with teacher education programs that have not responded on a large scale to the necessity of preparing teachers for diversity in student populations, partly because their own faculties are also predominantly white, middle class and don't always recognize the need.

The urban context as well as the difference in racial/ethnic backgrounds, also causes preservice and new teachers to worry about working in schools that are heavily Hispanic. The majority of Hispanic children are in urban school districts, even though more are enrolling in suburban and small town districts as well. Most teachers come from suburban school districts and they are anxious to teach in schools like the ones they are used to. In one study of preservice teachers in the upper Midwest, preservice teachers were asked about their preference for student teaching placements. Sixty-four percent indicated they wanted to be placed in majority white, suburban schools (Terrill & Mark, 2000). They expected higher levels of discipline problems, lower levels of parental support, and lower levels of motivation if they were placed in African American or Hispanic schools. Yet, 52 percent had never spent any time in classrooms with African American and Hispanic students so they were making choices without personal experience with these students. Regardless of what kinds of schools preservice teachers want to teach in, the reality is that the available teaching positions are in mostly urban districts that are heavily populated with Hispanic and other minority children. Even so, the "mismatch" or disonance in the racial/ethnic make up of teachers in the United States and the urban school districts does not have to be a problem. Much depends on how preservice and inservice teachers perceive their context and what their beliefs are about urban schools.

Research about Preservice Teachers' Beliefs about Hispanic Students

Although there are relatively few studies that explore how preservice teachers view Hispanic students specifically, those that have been conducted indicate that most white, middle class preservice teachers demonstrate little interest and tend to be afraid of teaching in schools that are predominantly Hispanic. Two factors in particular seem to worry preservice teachers about teaching in heavily Hispanic schools: (1) they have concerns about language barriers and (2) they know less about Hispanic populations than about other racial/ethnic minorities. The study referenced above (Terrill & Mark, 2000) asked preservice students about their comfort level in teaching different groups of children—they were least comfortable in a predominantly Hispanic school. The biggest worry for preservice teachers in that study was that they would not be able to communicate with students in Spanish. Interestingly, they said they would be open to taking Spanish so they could communicate with Hispanic parents and students, yet when asked their preferences, the school with a high percentage of Hispanic students was their last choice. The few teacher candidates who did want to teach in Hispanic schools indicated they already had some language proficiency in Spanish. Other studies also indicate that non-Hispanic preservice teachers believe they will have communication problems because of language differences (Groulx, 2001) and that they are not prepared to learn another language to communicate with students.

Anxiety over not speaking the language of students is understandable, but teachers need to remember they do have English proficiency and one of the most important things Spanish-dominant students need to learn is English. Preservice teachers may be unwilling or unable to use Spanish to communicate with students, but it would be reasonable to expect that they would be open to teaching English as a Second Language (ESL) to Spanish speakers. The concern about Spanish seems to drive thoughts about teaching ESL away though. Few studies address preservice teachers' willingness to learn how to teach ESL to Spanish speakers, but in our experience in teacher education, most preservice teachers want to learn methods of teaching ESL. They have a sense that knowing how to teach ESL will be advantageous to them in looking for a job. In at least one study, preservice teachers indicated they were open to learning to teach language minority children when they described experiences with non-English speakers and indicated they "felt good" whenever they were able to help children learn English (Griego Jones, 2002). Most non-Hispanic preservice teachers, however, do not anticipate having to teach children from non-English language backgrounds, assuming perhaps that these children will be taught by bilingual and/or English as a Second Language teachers. The "language issue" seems to be the most widely perceived problem or obstacle when preservice teachers consider the possibility of teaching Hispanic children. But, it is a misplaced worry. Most Hispanic children speak and understand English and those who don't can be taught by monolingual English speaking teachers through ESL.

Foreigners

The next biggest concern for preservice teachers is their belief about the "foreign aspect" of Hispanic students. Preservice teachers tend to make assumptions that the values of Hispanics are different from theirs because they come from foreign countries. There seems to be an impression that Hispanic populations are a new phenomenon in this country, even though Hispanic people colonized parts of the United States (Southwest and Puerto Rico) long before these areas became part of the United States. The percentage of Hispanics born in the United States is generally greater than the percentage of foreign born Hispanics even though those percentages have varied over the years. At the turn of the millenium, because of increased immigration in the 1990s, there was a higher percentage of foreign born Hispanics than ever before and this may have contributed to the belief that Hispanic students are foreign. Still, the majority of Hispanic students are born *in* the United States and the majority *are* proficient in English.

Segregation

One reason there are misconceptions about Hispanic children is that they are the most segregated student population in the country. They are more likely to attend schools where there are fewer "other" student groups than any other racial/ethnic group. The majority of Hispanic students are in California, Texas, New Mexico, Arizona, and on the east coast in New York and Florida. Midwest states like Illinois also have very large Hispanic populations. In these states, Hispanic students tend to be concentrated in urban schools, not spread around throughout all districts. Therefore, they have had fewer contacts with white suburban students who make up the majority of prospective teachers.

Media

The media has also consistently ignored Hispanics in television, movies, and the press except for negative stereotypes (Martinez, 2001) so preservice teachers have not had the opportunity to learn as much about Hispanics through the media. This was starting to change in the late 1990s as businesses in particular began to be aware of the economic implications of the demographic shift that made Hispanics the largest minority group in the United States. The cover story of the July 12, 1999 issue of *Newsweek* magazine, called Latin USA, described how young Hispanics, sometimes called *Generation Ñ*, were changing America through a quiet cultural revolution, particularly in large urban areas. Latin music and art in cities like

Miami, Los Angeles, New York, and Chicago were part of the cultural scene and enjoyed by everyone, not just Hispanics. By 2000, Hispanics, as the largest minority group in the United States had increased economic and political clout, which began affecting advertising, marketing, and corporate recruiting and hiring.

Bottom Line for the Teacher

Beliefs play a critical role in how preservice teachers learn how to teach as well as how they develop as teachers in their own classrooms. Teacher education must attend to the beliefs prospective teachers come with when they enter teacher preparation. It is true that teachers' beliefs *alone* do not account for the success or failure of Hispanic children in American public schools. There are a number of factors that have combined to create the situation in schools. As Sonia Nieto states in *Affirming Diversity*, "a constellation of attitudes, behaviors, and structures and a mismatch between home and school expectations all work together to produce success or failure" (Nieto, 1992, p. 31). Nevertheless, there has not been enough attention paid to the beliefs teachers bring with them about minority children in teacher education programs.

To expect children to make all the adjustments to differences puts all the burden on the "different" students. The students are not in charge of the classroom and what happens in it, the teacher is. Children cannot be expected to understand where the teacher is coming from and to understand how values and expectations of the teacher may be different from theirs and those of their parents. So, it is up to the *teacher* to be the one who can make the cultural leaps and adjustments. It is the teacher's professional responsibility to facilitate the learning in the classroom for all children.

EXERCISES FOR REFLECTION

The following questions are to get you thinking about the main topics of this chapter, about your knowledge and beliefs relating to your own cultural backgrounds and to Hispanic populations. Use these questions and add your own, to learn more about what you believe and how you think *and* about what you may need to change in order to teach Hispanic students effectively.

1. **Beliefs and knowledge about my own cultural group.** What do I know about my own roots? Why is important to know about own history and roots? Am I just American? What ethnic/racial groups are in my background? What

does American mean? What, in my unique heritage, has contributed to the American culture?

2. **Beliefs and knowledge about others.** What contact have I had with people different than my own family? What kinds of differences? How did I feel when I had contact with people of a different cultural group? How did I learn what I know about cultural groups other than my own?

3. **Beliefs about Hispanic students.** What is the difference between knowledge and beliefs? Write down all you *know* about Hispanic populations. Where/how did you learn this? Who or what influenced what you know about Hispanics?

   What do you *believe* about Hispanic populations? Students? Where did your beliefs come from? Who do you know (friends, teachers, movie stars, singers, politicians, etc.) that is Hispanic? What do you admire about them? What do you not admire about them? Are these people Mexican American, Puerto Rican, Cuban, or come from another Hispanic group?

4. **Beliefs about equity in schooling for Hispanic students.** How would you respond to these statements written by college juniors majoring in education and learning to be teachers? Do you agree or disagree with the following statements?

   a. "Teachers subconsciously or consciously expect less from minorities and/or low socioeconomic students...which after years of being treated that way in school leads to a self-fulfilling prophecy."

   b. "Ethnic groups are treated equally in schools but are not taught equally."

SUGGESTED ACTIVITIES

1. **Brainstorming stereotypes.** Have all class members write, without talking with each other, a list of all the stereotypes they can think of associated with the major racial/ethnic groups (African American, American Indian, Asian American, Euro-American, Hispanic American). Compile the lists under each racial/ethnic category, writing each word, phrase, even if they are mentioned more than once. Distribute the five lists to all members of the class and discuss. Prompts for discussion can be questions like: What are the most common stereotypes of each group? Are they positive or negative? Where do you suppose they come from? Why do people believe these things about any given group? Is there any evidence that the beliefs are true?

2. **Typebusters projects.** When preservice and inservice teachers recognize that beliefs may be stereotypes, they may want to "break down" the stereotypes within their classrooms. Projects that target getting accurate information about specific racial/ethnic groups can be "typebusters." Learning accurate, factual information about other cultural groups can dispel stereotypes and allows students to understand others as people, good and bad. It helps students to see how people are similar in their needs, desires, and behaviors. It shows

differences as artifacts of environment, pressures, and needs that different people in different places have, not as inherent good or bad traits. In education foundations classes, students have sometimes researched specific topics or stereotypes on our lists and presented their "evidence" to the class, playing the role of "typebusters" just as "ghostbusters" went into haunted houses to rid them of ghosts.

RESOURCES FOR CULTURAL DIVERSITY

Delpit, L. (1995). *Other people's children.* New York: The New Press.

Derman-Sparks, L., & Phillips, C. B. (1997). *Teaching/learning anti-racism.* New York: Teachers College Press.

Grant, C. A., & Gomez, M. L. (2001). *Campus and classroom: making schooling multicultural* (2nd ed.) Upper Saddle River, NJ: Prentice-Hall, Inc.

Howard, G. R. (1999). *We can't teach what we don't know.* New York: Teachers College Press.

Paley, V. G. (1979). *White teacher.* Cambridge, MA: Harvard University Press.

REFERENCES

Cabello, B., & Davis-Burstein, N. (1995). Examining teachers' beliefs about teaching culturally diverse classrooms. *Journal of Teacher Education, 46* (4), 285–294.

Fang, Z. (1996). A review of research on teacher beliefs and practices. *Educational Research, 38* (1), 47–65.

Gomez, M. L. (1994). Teacher education reform and prospective teachers' perspectives on teaching "other peoples" children. *Teaching and Teacher Education, 10* (3), 319–334.

Gomez, M. L., & Tabachnick, B. R. (1992). Telling teaching stories. *Teaching Education, 4* (2), 129–138.

Griego Jones, T. (2002). Relationships between preservice teachers' beliefs about second language learning and prior experiences with non-English speakers. In *Teacher training and effective pedagogy in the context of student diversity.* Information Age Publishing, Inc.

Groulx, J. G. (2001). Changing preservice teacher perceptions of minority schools. *Urban Education, 36* (1), 60–92.

Larmer, B. (1999, July 12). Latino America. *Newsweek, 48–51.*

Leland, J., & Chambers, V. (1999, July 12). Generation N. *Newsweek, 52–58.*

Lortie, D. C. (1975). *Schoolteacher: A sociological study.* Chicago: The University of Chicago Press.

Martinez, O. J. (2001). *Mexican-origin people in the United States.* Tucson, AZ: The University of Arizona Press.

Montecinos, C., & Rios, F. A. (1999). Assessing preservice teachers' zones of concern and comfort with multicultural education. *Teacher Education Quarterly,* summer 1999.

Nespor, J. (1987). The role of beliefs in the practice of teaching. *Journal of Curriculum Studies, 19* (4), 317–328.

Nieto, S. (1992). *Affirming diversity.* New York: Longman.
Pajares, M. (1992). Teachers' beliefs and educational research: Cleaning up a messy construct. *Review of Educational Research, 62* (3), 307–332.
Richardson, V. (1996). The role of attitudes and beliefs in learning to teach. In J. Sikula (Ed.), *Handbook of research on teacher education* (pp. 102–119). New York: Macmillan.
Terrill, M., & Mark, D. L. H. (2000). Preservice teachers' expectations for schools with children of color and second-language learners. *Journal of Teacher Education, 51* (2), 149–155.
Zimpher, N., & Ashburn, E. (1992). Countering parochialism in teacher candidates. In M. Dilworth (Ed.), *Diversity in teacher education: New expectations* (pp. 40–62). San Francisco: Jossey-Bass.

CHAPTER

3 The History of Mexico and Other Hispanic Countries

This chapter covers the following topics:

- Patterns of oppression
- Life before Columbus
- The coming of the "old world"
- Important events for Mexico
- Mexico and the United States
- Important events in the history of Puerto Rico, Cuba, and the Dominican Republic

You cannot know a group's culture if you don't know the group's history. This is because what has happened in the past affects how a culture sees the world today and consequently how they act. A person doesn't even have to know their history for them to feel the effects of it. Even after four or five generations, people are still influenced by their ancestors' cultures even though they may have limited knowledge of those cultures (Glazer and Moynihan, 1990).

History is not only a documentation of events but is also a matter of perspective. The historical events presented in this chapter would certainly be viewed differently by the other countries involved: Spain, France, the United States, and others. However, our main concern in this chapter is the effects of historical events on Mexico.

It is impossible to cover the history of one country in a single chapter, much less the history of several countries. Thus the information in this chapter provides you with highlights and assists you in identifying patterns primarily for Mexico.

Background: Oppression and Violence

The history of Mexico and other Latin countries since 1492 has been one of oppression. The particulars may vary but the outcome was the same.

Merriam's Collegiate Dictionary defines *oppression* as an unjust or cruel exercise of authority or power, something that oppresses especially in being an unjust or excessive exercise of power. This is an excellent description of many of the events you will review in this chapter.

Perhaps one of the most misunderstood aspects of oppression is the effect on its victims because oppression that is clearly inexorable and invincible does not [generally] give rise to revolt but rather to submission (Simone Weil, a French philosopher, 1979). You may wonder why these oppressed groups didn't revolt more often. However, you come to this question with a perspective that is a product of a free society.

There are a variety of ways to oppress a culture. Athough Pablo Freire's observations pertain to oppression in contemporary society, his "truths" are timeless and his observations appropriate to the examination of the colonization of Latin America:

> the oppressed, who have adapted to the structure of domination...and became resigned to it, are inhibited from waging the struggle for freedom (Freire, 1997, p. 29).

An excellent visual example of this oppression can be found in Mérida, Mexico, (the capital of the Yucatan state) where a large percentage of the population are Mayans—the indigenous people of that area. Francisco de Montejo founded Mérida in 1542 on the site of a Mayan city he destroyed. And in this charming colonial city, one can view two statues of Montejo. What is significant and telling is that Montejo is standing on the head of a Mayan Indian and that Montejo himself commissioned this work. In other words, he recognized his wealth, which was considerable, was a result of his cruel and unjust treatment of the Mayans. He not only recognized the oppression but saw it as a desirable, something to be proud of.

> As unpleasant and uncomfortable as they [the facts of Hispanic oppression] may be, these aspects of human relations in the history of our nation must be faced squarely by anyone earnestly desirous of achieving a fuller understanding of the historical conditions of Mexican origin people [and other Hispanics]. (Martinez, 2001, p. 51)

As you read this chapter please note the acts of oppression and violence experienced by the indigenous and Hispanic populations.

AUTHOR'S NOTE **Mary Lou Fuller**

When I was a student in an Arizona high school, Mexican history was not part of the curriculum. Although I lived on the south side of the Gila river (formerly a part of Mexico) I saw no connection between Mexican history and my life. Many names of rivers and mountains, and so on were Spanish, the architecture of the area had been influenced by Mexico, as was the food we ate (pinto beans were a staple for many families). But most importantly, the influence of the large Mexican American population—many whose ancestors had lived in the area before it became part of the United States—was not recognized.

I didn't understand that the history of Mexico was also my history and the history of my community. I believe now that my understanding of my world would have been richer and more insightful had I had this knowledge. But even sadder was that my Hispanic classmates didn't know of the wonderful contributions made to the area by their families—and nothing has changed in the sense that Mexican history is still not part of the curriculum.

With the increasing number of Mexican and other Hispanic students in our schools, Mexican history must become part of every teacher's world.

Pre-Columbian Period

The history for Mexico and other Hispanic countries did not begin with the arrival of the conquistadors or the recognition of the new world by Europe. These Hispanic societies had a rich and varied history for many centuries before the arrival of the Spanish. Text books often present these multiple societies as having had a single common culture. While this might make viewing these pre-Columbian populations easier, it also presents a simplistic and false picture. There were, and are, heterogenous cultures at all the geographic sites (e.g., Columbia, Cuba, Puerto Rico, Mexico). Mexico (or better, the land mass that is now called Mexico) is a good example of the diversities of culture in a given geographic area.

Consider the period just prior to the Cortés invasion of Mexico, and you will have an excellent example of the variety of cultures in a given geographic area. During this period the Mayan Indians, who at one time had been the most highly-developed culture of the area, were now past their cultural and political prime. Formerly they had been known as great artists, astronomers, architects, and mathematicians and had identified the concept of zero prior to the "old" world—a brilliant mathematical contribution. At the same time, in what is now Baja California, there was a culture made up of people whose lives were similar to people of the stone age. And on the opposite end of the continuum were the Aztecs who were exceptional urban planners (perhaps the best in the world), well educated (their knowledge, kept in elaborate codices, contained not only their cosmology but also medicinal, astronomical, and historical information), and their architecture was so innovative and sophisticated that they were considered to be the most advanced culture of the period in what is now Mexico. There were numerous other cultures too, each with its own uniqueness.

Looking at what was happening in other parts of the world helps put pre-Columbian cultures in historical perspective. During the Mayan classical period (300 A.D. to 900 A.D.), Palenque was far in advance of Europe in the sphere of public health. They had a sewer system that consisted of stone troughs that ran through buildings and was fed by a continuous stream of water that transported waste from the area.

Before the roads of the city of Rome were paved, Teotihuacán, a large religious complex of pyramids and ceremonial buildings was perhaps the most beautiful city in the world and home to approximately 50,000 inhabitants. The inhabitants of Teotihuacán were precursors to the Aztecs who later conquered them, took over their land, and claimed it for themselves.

There is a danger in romanticizing the pre-Columbian period as one of harmony and peace with all things being just. Cultures of that period and place exhibited the characteristics of cultures over history. Thus, while some were very productive in the arts, medicine, law, education, and so forth, they also exhibited the same foibles as other cultures throughout history.

The Arrival of Spain

1519, Spanish Conquistadors Defeat Aztecs

In 1517 Hernán Cortés and 509 men landed on the east coast of what is now Mexico. Cortés burned his boats to discourage mutiny. The trip from the Atlantic to the Aztec capital city of Tenochtitlán was an arduous one requiring travel through difficult terrain (mountains, swamps, etc.), carrying supplies as well as cannons and other instruments of war. Their horses, the first in the "new world," were a definite asset. People often question how such a small band of soldiers could defeat a much larger population on their home ground, and there are a number of reasons that contributed to the Aztec's defeat. Two primary reasons are first that Cortés's men were equipped with superior instruments of war, and second that many Aztecs died of smallpox—a disease brought by the Spaniards and to which the Aztecs had no natural immunity. Other factors included alliances with the Aztec's enemies who, when they saw how effective horses and guns were, decided to join Cortés in order to attack their main enemies, the Aztecs. Indigenous people also had a legend of a god that was to return to the Aztecs and some felt that might be in the embodiment of Cortés.

Starting with Cortés, Mexico's history continued as one of oppression that primarily evidenced itself through fights for land, a fight that continues today (e.g., the Zapatistas, in the state of Chiapas). It was, and is, the universal struggle between the haves and have-nots. When the conquistadors arrived at the shore of a desired land, they would read a proclamation in Spanish claiming the land for Spain in the name of Queen Isabel and King Ferdinand. They would then plant the Spanish flag and consider the land legally the property of Spain.

The minerals, precious metals and gems, and agricultural products became an important source of wealth for Spain and for the conquistadores. A part of this exploitation was the human element of this economic equation. Large numbers of indigenous people were enslaved and forced to work in the fields and mines. Still others, although not officially slaves, lived in poverty as peons serving the needs of large landholders in much the same way as serfs served the Lords of the Manor during the medieval period. Three centuries of Spanish rule followed and the indigenous population of Mexico was reduced from 25 million to less than six million.

The contact between the indigenous populations and the Europeans resulted in a new culture—the mestizo culture of Mexico. The majority of Mexican people are a combination of Spanish and indigenous groups. All of these cultures made both positive and negative contributions to one another and over time, became blended into the national culture.

1810, Father Miguel Hidalgo Unleashes the Mexican Movement for Independence from Spain

Dissatisfaction with Spain was ongoing for many years among the natives of Mexico—Creole (Spaniards born in Mexico), mestizos, and indigenous groups. All of these Mexicans revolted and declared their independence from Spain. A Creole Catholic priest, Father Miguel Hidalgo of a small parish consisting of indigenous and mestizo citizens, is credited with "the call to arms" with his Grito de Dolores (Cry of Dolores) on September 16, 1810. From the pulpit he said,

> My children, a new dispensation comes to us today. Are you ready to receive it? Will you be free? Will you make an effort to recover from the hated Spaniards the land stolen from your fathers 300 years ago?

He then proclaimed, "Mexicans! Long live Mexico! Death to the gachupines!"

Hidalgo and Ignacio Allende (a Creole soldier), led a ragtag legion armed with sticks, hay forks, and so on to retake Mexico and form communal lands. However, the battle for independence would last for 11 years and take more than 600,000 lives.

1821, Mexico Wins Independence from Spain

Although Mexico won its independence from Spain it continued to deal with political interference from other countries in Europe and the United States.

1848, Cinco de Mayo

After independence from Spain other European countries became interested in Mexico. The French attempted to assume control of Mexico but were unsuccessful. A decisive battle in the struggle against the French took place in Pueble on May 5 (Cinco de Mayo). Since then, Cinco de Mayo is a celebration of the battle where a poorly equipped and trained Mexican army defeated the larger French army, which was assumed to be superior.

1910, Mexican Revolution, a Long and Bloody Civil War

Once again the "haves" and "have-nots" were at war, but instead of the mestizos, indigenous people, and the Creoles fighting Spain for independence that was to provide land for all. The Creoles were now the land owners and the mestizos and indigenous people were still living oppressed and impoverished lives. They still lacked land and continued to be an exploited population.

The Mexican Revolution was complicated by a variety of players, politics, and motivations. Again, many of the troops were untrained, poorly equipped, and ill financed. The rebels destroyed railroads and most of the nation's crops and livestock, unleashing a food shortage that led to mass starvation and uncontrolled epidemics. Homes were destroyed and more than a million people lost their lives. Again, the poor were the victims of this revolution and were hurt both by those who claimed to represent them and those who wanted them to maintain their position of servitude. The misery caused by this revolution resulted in the first major wave of Mexicans coming to the United States.

Professional Moment

The Old Gringo, starring Gregory Peck, Jane Fonda, and Jimmy Smits, gives an excellent picture of what the Mexican Revolution was about. It clearly shows the differences between the haves and have-nots (the oppressor and the oppressed). As you watch this movie please note a least four of the contrasts between the Creole and the mestizos' lives. Share and discuss them with your class members.

The United States and Mexico

At this point in history Mexico had been looted of much of its natural and human resources to outside entities. The United States became actively interested in Mexico when a number of U.S. citizens moved to Tejas (Texas), a part of Mexico, and became citizens of Mexico. The interest of these expatriates was not political but rather, land. And that, too, was in the interest of the United States.

1836, The Alamo

"Remember the Alamo!" is a cry that seems to resonate patriotism. We have all heard it and yet few understand it.

Events leading up to the Alamo were neither simple nor linear. Texas was a sparsely settled part of Mexico. Sam Austin's father (Moses), was given permission by the Mexican government to settle Americans in Texas as long as they became Mexican citizens and followed the laws of Mexico, converted to Catholicism, and agreed not to have slaves, although the last was almost immediately broken by Austin and others.

Sam Austin continued his father's endeavors when Moses Austin died. The Austins were, in essence, land developers who were motivated by business interests. Sam Austin sold each Anglo farmer he recruited 117 acres and each rancher 4,428 acres while he kept 100,000 acres for himself. The number of former Americans living in Texas as Mexican citizens reached more than 50,000.

The United States saw some economic opportunities in Texas and offered the Mexican President, Santa Anna, one million dollars for Texas. This, and a misunderstanding when the citizens of this Mexican territory asked to become a Mexican state, caused Santa Anna to act in an ill-considered manner. He jailed Austin for 18 months and refused all of the requests of the territory, which resulted in Austin and others wanting to secede and form an independent country. All of these events set the stage for the Alamo.

The Texans' military (made up of both Anglos and Mexicans) seized a Mexican garrison full of supplies and then raided a military supply depot at the Alamo. In a state of humiliation, Mexico granted Texas independence. Soon afterwards, Santa Anna and an army of thousands started north to reclaim its lost territory. Due to a miscalculation as to where Santa Anna and his troops would enter the territory, the Alamo was vastly under staffed and although the 182 soldiers fought valiantly for five days, they suffered a crushing defeat. This might have seemed like the end of Texans' independence except that Sam Houston and his Texas army (they initially selected the wrong battlefield) proceeded to the Alamo area and attacked Santa Anna crying, "Remember the Alamo." They were victorious. Although Houston had fewer troops than Santa Anna, when the smoke from the cannons cleared, 600 of Santa Anna's men lay dead while only six Texans died. The Texans had won their independence and Sam Houston was elected their country's first president.

Contrary to popular belief, these battles had nothing to do with the United States. The territory (Texas) was Mexican, the Texans were citizens of Mexico, and it was a Mexican war.

The cry "Remember the Alamo" was a term used in relation to Mexico—and as a threat. Unfortunately it was generalized as a threat against Texas Mexicans who, for the most part, had supported Texas's bid for independence and had fought with Houston against Mexico.

Mexicans in the United States have had limited opportunities to share in the political and monetary wealth. As with the African American population, Mexican Americans have often had their civil rights violated. Some Mexicans were hung by vigilantes, lived in segregated communities, and attended segregated schools. It is a long and sad story of human rights infringement.

1845, Manifest Destiny

Before you can understand the following events, you must understand the term "manifest destiny" and its implications. In the summer of 1845, an article appeared in the *United States Magazine and Democratic Review* that put into words what many Americans already believed, that "our manifest destiny overspread the continent allotted by providence for the free development of our multiplying destiny." Or as Himilce Novas observes, "manifest destiny was an Anglo version of the national supremacy theory and justified the desire on the part of the United States to extend the borders from sea to shining sea "(1991, p. 72). And to give this self-proclaimed right legitimacy it was labeled as the will of God. This was the basis for the illegal expansion of our borders into Mexico, and the appropriation of the land of the American Indians—all this was justified as the United States' manifest destiny.

1836–1845, United States Annexed Texas

Texas was recognized by several nations as an independent country, including the United States. However, in 1836, due to a multitude of problems, Texas asked to be annexed by the United States. The United States was facing the problem of slavery, and with the states equally divided between free and slave, admitting Texas with its slaves would have tipped the balance. Texas was admitted to the United States on December 29, 1845, as the twenty-eighth state, with slavery permitted. Texas seceded from the United States and fought on the side of the Confederacy in 1861.

These events are especially important because the question of slavery was one of the factors leading to Mexican-American War.

1846, United States Declared War on Mexico

Mexico smarted from the annexation of Texas by the United States, an action that was seen by Mexico as an act of aggression. In addition, Mexicans were fearful that the United States wanted to acquire more of their land, and indeed did so. Mexico, after their experience with Texas, took serious steps to stop immigration from the United States into Mexico. The situation between the two nations grew even more tense when President James Polk, using "manifest destiny" as his justification, declared that he had every intent of acquiring California, that indeed, belonged to Mexico. Polk started with an offer to buy California, and to help the Mexican President understand the full implications of this request, he sent General Zachary Taylor to Texas to bivouac along the Rio Grande river. The unspoken message was obvious: If you don't sell us part of your country there are other ways to acquire it. Mexico declined Polk's offer and the United States declared war on Mexico on May 13, 1846. A year and a half later, Mexico acceded to U.S. demands and signed the Treaty of Guadalupe Hidalgo.

1848, Treaty of Guadalupe-Hidalgo; End of the Mexican-American War

While we tend to think of treaties as dry, legalistic documents, the treaty of Guadalupe Hidalgo was one of subterfuge and intrigue. Although Mexico thought there was only one treaty, there were actually two—the one signed by the Mexicans and the other signed by Congress. Before ratifying the treaty, and without notifying Mexico, the U.S. Congress deleted those items it found objectionable. Mexico lost a third of its land as a result of this treaty.

On February 1, 1848, the people of the land in question were citizens of Mexico and on February 2, 1848, without moving an inch, they became citizens of the United States with laws, language, and customs that were foreign to most. They were immigrants in what had been their native land; indeed, many of the formerly Mexican families had lived on the designated land for more generations than their families could remember.

Among other things, the treaty provided citizenship to those Mexicans of the area and they were also promised that their ownership of land and other properties would be protected. Nevertheless, many of the Mexicans lost their land because even though they'd lived there for generations. They sometimes did not have a deed, but often their deeds had been issued by the Mexican or Spanish governments and were not honored by the United States. While this was fine under Mexican law, it was not U.S. law, and the Mexican land owner was apt to be a victim of the politics of the two countries.

An interesting side note: The discovery of gold in California was kept a secret until after the signing of the treaty. It is unlikely that Mexico would have signed if they had been aware of the potential wealth. A few days after the signing the country and the world knew of the discovery, and multitudes were off to California—now part of the United States.

1853, Gadsden Purchase

In 1853 James Gadsden brokered an agreement allowing the United States to purchase a strip of land along the Gila River in southern Arizona and New Mexico. The Gadsden Purchase consisted of 45,532 square miles of an area rich with minerals and thus opened the possibility of expanded railroad routes for the United States. Again the Mexicans were assured the right to their land, but once again, these rights were not strictly enforced.

Mexico was in a difficult situation for concerning the Gadsden purchase because they once again had no choice but to sign the treaty or to face another war with the United States—a war they could not afford and could not win.

1929–2001

These years have seen a pattern of disregard for Mexico and Mexican citizenship that runs through the United States' relationship with Mexico, a pattern that often extended to U.S. citizens of Mexican ethnicity as described in the following paragraphs.

Early 1900s—Immigrants

Due to the expansion of irrigation agriculture in the Southwest, agriculture grew rapidly and there was a great need for cheap labor. This need coincided with the Mexican Revolution so that many Mexicans displaced by the ravages of war found employment in the United States. They worked in the fields, in the mines, for the railroads, in the cotton, sugar, and beet fields, and in industry. Indeed, they made a substantial contribution to the economic growth of the Southwest.

1929–1935, Thousands of Mexicans Were Returned to Mexico without Legal Process

This was during the Great Depression, and most Americans felt the effects of the economic decline. Unemployment went from four million to thirteen million and pay from 35 cents an hour to 15 cents. And like all minorities, Mexican Americans were among the first laid off when jobs disappeared. The situation became so serious that on taking office, President Franklin Roosevelt initiated work projects specifically for this population. However, there was strong anti-Mexican sentiment with many Anglo Americans feeling that all Mexicans, regardless of their citizenship, were foreigners and were taking jobs from the "real" Americans. The result was that without regard for civil rights, about half a million Mexicans were deported back to Mexico. Some were illegal immigrants, of course, but many were citizens of the United States, and, indeed, some came from families who had lived in the United States for a hundred years or more. Needless to say, these people felt betrayed and were bitter toward the United States.

1942–1947, The Bracero Program

Due to the lack of farm workers during World War II, the United States authorized Mexicans to work in the United States temporarily. Due to the draft during World War II there was a serious shortage of men to work on farms, particularly at harvest time. Mexicans were allowed into the United States for this seasonal work. The second Bracero program during the Vietnam War era was similar to the first in that field workers were needed.

1954, Operation Wetback,[1] a Massive Deportation Program of Undocumented Workers

The need for Mexican workers had decreased and again people who had established homes, become members of communities, and whose children attended schools and who may well have been born in the United States, were sent back to Mexico. Only a few were afforded due process and many

[1]A name for an immigrant that illegally enters this country. At one time, the Rio Grande flowed and many immigrants swam the river, hense the term *wetback*.

citizens of the United States who were Mexican were arrested and harassed. One million people were deported as a result of Operation Wetback.

1965, Grape Strike

The importance of this strike was the high visibility of Cesar Chavez and the United Farm Workers who in turn drew attention to the appalling conditions of the farm workers and the degree to which they were exploited by the agri-businessmen. The first farm worker's union was formed in California in 1927, and when union members attempted to strike, violence, intimidation, and deportations were used to end the protest.

The grape strike covered the same issues as earlier strikers—poor pay and deplorable working conditions. And this time, however, strikes were successful in bringing the plight of the migrant workers to the public's attention. The success of the strike was due, in part, to the support of public figures (entertainers, politicians, etc.) whose presences gave the strike and the issues it addressed a high profile.

Court Cases and Educational Rights of Hispanic Children

There were many court cases which addressed educational inequities for Hispanic children. In fact, the first successful legal challenge to school segregation in the United States was *Alvarez v. Lemon Grove* (1931) in which Mexican American parents challenged the Lemon Grove School District's plan to build separate schools for Mexican American children. *Mendez v. Westminster* (1946) preceded *Brown v. Board of Education* by a decade and was the first *federal* court decision in the area of school segregation and *Mendez* ended de jure segregation in California. Many others followed across the country. For a comprehensive treatment of the legal history related to Hispanic student rights, see Valencia and San Miguel's "From the Treaty of Guadalupe Hidalgo to 'Hopwood': The Educational Plight and Struggle of Mexican Americans in the Southwest."

The 1973 Supreme Court decision in *Keyes v. Denver School District* addressed the needs of desegregated Hispanic students, including the need for bilingual and English as a Second Language programs. This case is mentioned here because of the personal involvement of one of the authors of this book. The Court stated that a meaningful desegregation plan must not only physically integrate Hispanic students, but must also help them become proficient in English. In other words, bilingual education can be derived as a component of a desegregation remedy, but it cannot be the remedy for a segregated school system (Wells, 1989).

AUTHOR'S NOTE **Mary Lou Fuller**

This is truly an author's note for it is one author sharing important information about the other author—Toni Griego Jones. Toni was a major figure in the Keyes case. In an attempt to ensure a better education for Hispanic children in Denver she, over a period of several years, donated her talents and time. Many of the strategy sessions were held in her living room, and she became known as the person who had the best understanding of the educational implications and was sought out as the authority on the legal implications of the Keyes case. She deserves not only our recognition but also our appreciation.

1986, The Immigration Reform and Control Act

This act was designed to control the entrance of undocumented workers and imposed severe penalties. Considering that the number of undocumented workers has increased significantly since this period suggests it did not meet it goals.

History of Cuba, Dominican Republic, and the Commonwealth of Puerto Rico

The history of Mexico, as with all countries, is unique and yet it shares many common experiences with other Hispanic countries in the hemisphere. Table 3.1 provides a brief history of three other Hispanic countries. Common acts of exploitation and oppression are identifiable and the effects of these historic events are still in evidence.

Summary

There are common identifiable patterns that emerge from the history of Mexico and other Hispanic countries—patterns of exploitation, oppression, and the disproportionate distribution of wealth (the haves and have-nots).

TABLE 3.1 Historical Overview of Puerto Rico, Cuba, and the Dominican Republic

Dates	Puerto Rico	Cuba	Dominican Republic
1400s	*1493.* Columbus's second voyage. Columbus noted in his journal how peaceful the indigenous were and how cooperative they had been. He took possession of the land in the name of Spain.	*1492.* Columbus wrote in his journal, "I have never seen anything so beautiful." He claimed the land in the name of Spain. It is estimated that there were about 100,000 natives upon Columbus's arrival; however, the Cubans, as the Puerto Ricans, were nearly decimated by European illnesses, overwork, and misuse.	*1492.* Columbus landed and established the first Spanish Colony in the new world. The natives welcomed him with gifts of gold. Consequently Columbus wrongly assumed that gold was plentiful on the island. *1496.* The Spanish royalty sent Columbus's brother to exploit and export the gold of the island to Spain. The city of Santa Domingo was established.
1500s	*1508.* Ponce de Leon was sent by Spain to look for gold. Although there was little gold, Ponce de Leon recognized the value of the beautiful harbor. Spain appointed him the first governor of Puerto Rico and he enslaved a great number of natives and so many died (illness, starvation, mistreatment, & exhaustion) that his work force was inadequate to his needs. During the 1500s sugar was planted and mills were built. *1513.* Ponce de Leon imported thousands of slaves from Africa and with them came smallpox.	*1511.* Spain with their desire for gold sent Diego Valdez to secure lands, form settlements, and find gold. Valdez was a wealthy land owner who had, through battle, secured large quantities of land. It became apparent that the wealth of Cuba lay in its rich land and strategic placement. It was a perfect stopping place for the conquistadors on their way to the Americas. The Spaniard brought African slaves to Cuba by the thousands.	

	1515. Of the 30,000 to 40,000 Taino that were present when Columbus arrived, 22 years later there were fewer than 4,000.		*1543.* The gold had been depleted and Spain's interest turned to the wealth of Mexico and Peru. Although some colonizers established plantations on the eastern part of the island.
1600s		*1607.* Havana is named the capital of Cuba.	*1697.* The western third of the island was ceded to France, who named it Saint Domingue. The French colonists imported thousands of slaves from Africa as most of the indigenous people had died of overwork, disease, starvation, etc.
1700s	*Mid-1700s.* Alijandro O'Riley, under the direction of Spain, was responsible for a period of growth. New towns, schools, and stone houses were built and commerce was streamlined.	*1715.* Spain created a monopoly (Factoria). They purchased all Cuban tobacco at fixed prices and sold it abroad.	*1795.* Spain relinquished the western two-thirds of the island to France.
1800s	*1823.* The United States, with James Monroe as president enacted the Monroe Doctrine. This forbade European expansion in the Americas.		*1804.* The African slaves revolted against the French colonists and declared the region an independent nation named Haiti. *1808.* The Spanish colonists of Santo Domingo were alarmed and reestablished rule. *1822.* The Haitians invaded Santo Domingo and ruled the island.

(continued)

TABLE 3.1 Continued

Dates	Puerto Rico	Cuba	Dominican Republic
1800s	*1870.* Political parties were formed. *1896.* End of Spanish American War. Puerto Rico was ceded to the United States.		*1844.* Led by the father of democracy, Juan Pablo Durante, the Spanish-speaking population of Santo Domingo declared their independence and named their country Dominican Republic.
1900	*1917.* President Woodrow Wilson signs the Jones Act, granting all Puerto Ricans U.S. citizenship. *1952.* The commonwealth of Puerto Rico elects to retain commonwealth status. *1993.* The people of Puerto Rico elect to retain commonwealth status.	*1902.* Cuba wins its independence and elects its first president, Thomas Estrada Palma. *1959.* Fulgenico Batista flees Cuba in the early dawn for safety in Spain and the rebels, led by Castro, assumed control. *1962.* President Kennedy announces that Russian atomic missile sites are being built in Cuba.	*1905.* President Teddy Roosevelt, using his corollary of the Monroe Doctrine, set up the United States as "police" in the Western hemisphere, including the Dominican Republic. *1906–1911.* Ramon Caceres was elected president. This was a period of modernization and growth. *1916.* After Caceres was assassinated President Woodward Wilson invaded the Dominican Republic to restore order. The United States remained until 1924. *1930.* Rafael Truijillo essentially stole the 1930 election. This was a long and violent dictatorship ending with his assassination in 1961. As dictator he accumulated $800 million. Human rights were all but nonexistent. He maintained a relationship with the United States and supplied sugar, etc., during the WWII. The United States was aware of these atrocities but did not intervene.

It is important to take a broad view of Hispanic history and not consider the past in isolation. We must consider the implication of the past on the present and for the future. If you consider the history of Hispanic cultures as an ongoing struggle for human rights, rather than segmenting it, battle by battle, or foreign exploitation by exploitation, it is easier to understand interconnectedness of the past, and present with the future.

The societal oppression of Hispanic populations still continues and often is perpetuated by our educational institutions in the United States. Among these institutions are the schools in the United States and as educators we are responsible for recognizing these areas of injustice and actively work to eliminate them.

EXERCISES FOR REFLECTION

1. Read the book, *The Mexican American Family Album*, by Dorothy Hoobler, Thomas Hoobler, and Henry G. Costner. The book makes history come alive through its fascinating narrative about real families and the numerous photographs which places human face on the events covered in this chapter.
2. Art is another way to learn about history and the artist Diego Rivera, using the medium of art, is a wonderful teacher. In the National Palace in Mexico City are murals which chronicle the history of Mexico, pre and post Columbian. Most libraries will have books with reproductions of these murals. Study the murals and note those events you can identify. Then read the description of the events depicted in the mural and make a time line of the events portrayed.
3. Interview a Mexican person sixty or older about his/her childhood. What events Do they remember? How have things changed? How are they the same?
4. As a class or as individuals watch the movie *The Mission* (Cast: Robert DeNiro, Jeremy Irons, 1986). Although this movie is historic in nature it provides insights into contemporary oppression. It's the story of a man of the cloth and a man of the sword who unite to shield a South American Indian tribe from brutal subjugation by eighteenth century colonial empires.
5. Divide the class into small groups and assign a period of history to each group. Have them identify, and then share with the class, what surprised and/or upset them.

RESOURCES FOR MEXICAN HISTORY

Carr, R. (1980). *Puerto rico: A colonial experiment*. New York: New York University Press.

Gann, L. H., & Duignan, P. (1986). *The Hispanics in the United States: A history*. Boulder, CO: Westview.

Gonzales, M. G. (2000). *Mexicanos: A history of Mexicans in the United States.* Bloomington: Indiana University Press.

Gonzales, M. G., & Gonzales, C. M. (2000). *En aquel entonces (In years gone by): Readings in Mexican-American history.* Bloomington: Indiana University Press.

Novas, H. (1998). *Everything you need to know about Latino history.* New York: Plume.

WEBSITES: HISPANIC HISTORY

Mexico

http://www.mexconnect.com/mex_/history.html

http://www.differentworld.com/mexico/common/pages/history.htm

http://www.ancientmexico.com/

Puerto Rico

http://www.geocities.com/TheTropics/3684/history.html

http://www.rainforestsafari.com/history.html

Cuba

http://www.emayzine.com/lectures/HISTOR~7.htm

http://historicaltextarchive.com/sections.php?op=viewarticle&artid=122

Dominican Republic

http://historicaltextarchive.com/sections.php?op=viewarticle&artid=362

REFERENCES

Freire, P. (1997). *Pedagogy of the oppressed.* New York: Continuum Publishing.

Glazer, N., & Moynihan, D. P. (1990). *Beyond the melting pot: The Negroes, Puerto Ricans, Jews, Italians, and Irish of New York*, 2nd ed., New York: Joint Center for Urban Studies.

Martinez, O. J. (2001). *Mexican-origin people in the United States: A topical history.* Tucson: University of Arizona Press.

Novas, H. (1998). *Everything you need to know about Latino history.* New York: Plume.

Weil, S. (1979). *Lectures on philosophy.* Cambridge, England: Cambridge University Press.

Wells, A. S. (1989). *Hispanic education in America: Separate and unequal.* New York: ERIC Clearinghouse on Urban Education. (ERIC/CUE Digest No. 59, ED316616)

CHAPTER

4 Language in the Hispanic Community

This chapter covers the following topics:

- Understanding the history of language usage in public schools
- The use of Spanish in schools
- Spanish and English usage within communities
- Bilingual education
- English as a Second Language programs

Language and the complexity of language use in Hispanic communities is such a critical variable in the education of Hispanic students. Many school districts believe that they have addressed the needs of Hispanic students when they develop bilingual or English as a Second Language programs. This erroneous belief is based on the assumption that a language barrier is the *only* reason many Hispanic students drop out of school or do not achieve well academically. This assumption is false. The high Hispanic dropout rates and underachievement are not just due to a language barrier. Other factors, such as the alienation of Hispanic students, high rates of poverty, ineffective teaching, misunderstandings, discrimination, and low expectations all contribute to the lack of academic success for Hispanic students. In fact, in many cases, Hispanic children who are proficient in English (sometimes only speak English) and not in bilingual programs drop out at higher rates and are at greater risk than those consistently enrolled in bilingual or ESL programs.

Language is a major factor in the academic success of all children and is certainly one of the critical factors in the education of Hispanic children. However, Hispanic children's native language may be Spanish or English, and in most cases, both languages are present in the socialization and daily lives of the children. Because of this linguistic complexity within the Hispanic community, language is a particularly important consideration for Hispanic populations—but not because it is the only, or even the major barrier to learning in U.S. classrooms.

Most Hispanic children are not in Bilingual Education and English as a Second Language programs, but these programs are discussed here because a significant number are, and because principles and practices found in bilingual/English as a Second Language classrooms can inform non-bilingual teachers about teaching second language learners. Also, because there is so much controversy associated with Bilingual and ESL programs, it is professionally helpful to have all educators understand the goals, approaches, and organization of these programs relative to Hispanic children.

In the past, immigrant groups have come to the United States in large numbers and then their numbers have dwindled. So, as they learned English, they lost their native languages. In the case of Hispanics, though, continuous immigration has maintained Spanish as a viable language. Even so, according to the 2000 census, the majority of Hispanics are fluent in English and many do not consider themselves to be proficient in Spanish. Many understand some Spanish phrases even if they are not able to converse in Spanish, and many use selected words sometimes mixing them with English words. Using some Spanish is often more a way of signaling a person's identification with the Hispanic community than needing to communicate in Spanish. The point is, there is a *range* of Spanish and English proficiency, from Spanish dominant, to varying degrees of bilingual, to monolingual English speakers. A brief history of languages, especially Spanish, in the United States can help explain the complexity of language for Hispanic populations.

Brief History of Languages in American Public Schools

A Multilingual Society

Before the arrival of Europeans in what is now the United States, there were more than 500 Native American languages spoken in North America, some of which are still used today, especially in the Southwest. Navajo, Hopi, and Tohono O'odham in particular are experiencing a renaissance as people are trying to preserve their cultural heritage by teaching these languages to their children. The native language of the Hawaiians is also being taught in schools after a time when it was endangered. When Europeans did arrive in North America in the 1500s, it was Spain that first colonized parts of what is now the United States (New Mexico, Arizona, Texas, California, Colorado, Florida, Puerto Rico) and firmly established Spanish in these areas where it continues to be a widely used language. Throughout the 1600s Spanish colonists continued to settle these areas while colonists from England and many other European nations settled along the eastern seaboard and Gulf Coast so that, at the time of the American Revolution in 1776, German as well as Scotch, Irish, Dutch, French, Swedish, Spanish, Portuguese, Danish, and Welsh were widely spoken in the thirteen colonies even though English was accepted as the dominant language of the newly formed United States (Andersson & Boyer, 1978; Castellanos, 1985; Crawford, 1989).

While Spanish colonization continued in the West, the U.S. government was established on the Eastern seaboard with English as the dominant language. The freedom to use other languages in public schools within the 13 states immediately became a political debate. Whenever a language minority group was large enough and politically powerful enough, it was able to insist that its language be used in private or public schooling. For example, because of the ongoing German immigration which made Germans the largest non-English group in the United States throughout the 1700s and 1800s, schools using German as the exclusive medium of instruction or in various combinations with English were common east of the Mississippi until the late 1800s.

Many immigrant groups also established their own religious schools to maintain their cultural values and were able to use their own languages as well as English for instruction. Since public schools were locally controlled, they too were responsive to political pressures of local ethnic communities. Local control of schools enabled various groups to incorporate their languages into the curriculum and make teaching their languages an accepted responsibility of the public schools in the United States. English was taught as a subject even if other languages were the primary medium of instruction, but the use of languages other than English in public schools has always been accompanied by public debate.

Spanish West and Southwest

When the United States acquired the Southwest from Mexico in 1848 and 1853, it also acquired an estimated 40 to 60 thousand Spanish speakers who became citizens overnight. These people had originally colonized for Spain and became Mexican citizens in 1821 when Spain lost Mexico in the Mexican War for Independence. In the 223 years that Spain owned what is now the Southwestern United States, Spanish speaking colonists continuously settled in northern New Mexico, southern Arizona, southern Texas, and California. Missions provided most of the schooling for colonists and Indians alike in the Spanish period. These schools used Spanish as the primary medium of instruction, but also used Indian languages as well. Bilingualism was a fairly common thing in Spanish societies. It did not then, nor does it now, have the political connotations that it does in American society where becoming proficient in a language other than English sometimes raises questions of national loyalty. Most of the missionaries learned the languages of their students although they absolutely taught the Spanish language as the official language to all people they converted.

When Mexico owned the Southwest from 1821–1848, it sent colonists northward in an effort to expand its settlements and fortify its position in the northern frontier. This resulted in relatively well populated areas (San Antonio, San Francisco, Los Angeles, and Santa Fe, for example) when the United States took over in 1848. This is an important point because we tend to think the American west was "empty" when settlers from Europe and the Eastern United States rushed westward. In fact, there were significant numbers of Native American languages and Spanish speakers in cities and rural farms and ranches when American settlers moved westward. Soon, where Spanish speaking populations had been the majority, they became the minority as they were overwhelmed with primarily non-Hispanic immigrants in search of gold and land.

The American expansion to the West and Southwest was often accompanied by confrontations between the Spanish speaking residents and the English speaking officials of the American government. This cultural and linguistic clash still manifests itself today in schools and other public arenas. Even though the Treaty of Guadalupe Hidalgo between the United States and Mexico guaranteed Spanish speaking residents the right to maintain their language and culture, this option was by and large disregarded by Americans in the establishment of American institutions, including schools.

Sometimes other languages besides English and Spanish were used in institutions when there were significant numbers of speakers of the languages. For example, when Colorado became a state, it had laws to conduct and publish official business in Spanish, English, and German. German was dropped, but the use of Spanish has seesawed back and forth since in legal and political debates. In the first years of U.S. rule (1848–1855) in the Southwest, public schools promoted the use of Spanish and included Mexican history and cultural heritage in the curriculum. This was possible because public schools were local institutions controlled by members of the local communities and many local communities were comprised primarily of Spanish/Mexican Americans. As Easterners moved in, they were intolerant of what they saw as "foreignisms" in the public schools and began to systematically "Americanize" the public schools themselves by outlawing Spanish. This process continued until the turn of the century although it happened with varying degrees of success. According to San Miguel and Valencia (1998) in an extensive review of language policy in the United States, "the subtraction of Spanish from the schools occurred in two phases...in the first phase, mostly during the 1850s, Spanish was usually only limited as a medium of instruction.... During the second phase, from 1870 to the early 1890s Spanish was prohibited in the schools."

In the 1850s, Texas and California received the greatest migration of Americans from the East and these newcomers quickly enacted legislation restricting the use of Spanish. New Mexico, on the other hand, had less migration from the East Coast except along the Santa Fe Trail and so remained predominantly Spanish speaking until the turn of the century. Anglo American officials in New Mexico were unsuccessful at enacting laws prohibiting Spanish because of the political strength of the predominantly Hispanic population. By late 1880s however, English-only legislation was passed in New Mexico as Anglo American anxieties about the influence and maintenance of Spanish as a dominant language increased. Since then, at various times, laws prohibiting the use of Spanish in schools have been passed, effectively excluding Spanish speaking students from instructional programs. These laws went so far as to punish children for speaking Spanish, thus further alienating Hispanic populations from American schools, especially those who were "here first."

Proliferation of Languages in the Twentieth Century

The immigration that brought languages other than English from Europe to the United States continued throughout the 1800s and 1900s. Immigration patterns changed in the late 1900s, however. Prior to 1848, German was the most widely spoken language other than English in the United States. Where the 1800s brought primarily Europeans, the 1900s brought many more Asian languages (Vietnamese, Laotian, Hmong, Cambodian), and more Spanish speakers from Cuba, Central and South America, the Domincan Republic, and the Caribbean. With the acquisition of the Southwest in 1848, later Puerto Rico in 1898, and Cuban refugees in the late 1950s and early 1960s, Spanish became the largest minority language in the United States. By 2001 the United States had one of the largest Spanish speaking populations in the world with over 17 million speakers. Table 4.1 ranks the 20 local education agencies (LEAs) according to the number of students identified as limited English proficient (LEP) enrolled in the 1993–1994 school year.

In 1990 there were an estimated 32 million people in the United States who used a language other than English at home (U.S. Census,

TABLE 4.1 Highest Numbers of Limited English Proficient Students

Rank	District	No. LEPs	Total Enrollment	% LEP
1.	Los Angeles, CA	291,527	639,129	45.6
2.	New York, NY	154,526	1,015,756	15.2
3.	Chicago, IL	57,964	409,499	14.2
4.	Dade County, FL	54,735	422,658	13.0
5.	Houston, TX	50,839	200,839	25.3
6.	Santa Ana, CA	33,540	48,407	69.3
7.	San Diego, CA	33,397	127,258	26.2
8.	Dallas, TX	31,522	142,810	22.1
9.	Long Beach, CA	26,042	76,783	33.9
10.	Fresno, CA	24,022	78,349	31.5
11.	Garden Grove, CA	17,673	41,664	42.9
12.	San Francisco, CA	17,673	61,631	28.7
13.	El Paso, TX	17,609	64,145	27.5
14.	Montebello, CA	14,988	32,321	46.4
15.	Glendale, CA	14,930	28,742	51.9
16.	Broward County, FL	14,622	236,885	6.2
17.	Boston, MA	14,518	59,613	24.4
18.	Oakland, CA	14,044	51,748	27.1
19.	Pomona, CA	13,381	29,880	44.8
20.	Sacramento, CA	12,290	49,997	24.0

U.S. Department of Education's Office of Bilingual Education and Minority Language Affairs (OBEMLA).

1990). For 17 million of them, Spanish was the other language. It is important for teachers to note that 77 percent of the 17 million who spoke Spanish at home also described themselves as using English well or very well. It is also informative for teachers to know that the languages represented in public schools are not necessarily the same languages represented in the general public. A study conducted by the U.S. Department of Education to describe the number and characteristics of limited English proficient (LEP) students during the 1991–1992 school year revealed the most common language groups among LEP students (see Table 4.2). Spanish is still the most common "other language," but the schools have many more Asian speakers than in the general public. After Spanish, most people claim to use French at home, but the second most widely used language in schools is Vietnamese.

Large urban school districts typically have 80–100 different languages represented in their student populations with Los Angeles and New York

TABLE 4.2 **Top 20 Language Groups in the United States**

Rank	Language Groups	No. LEP Students	% of LEP Students
1.	Spanish	1,682,560	72.9%
2.	Vietnamese	90,922	3.9
3.	Hmong	42,305	1.8
4.	Cantonese	38,693	1.7
5.	Cambodiam	37,742	1.6
6.	Korean	36,568	1.6
7.	Laotian	29,838	1.3
8.	Navajo	28,913	1.3
9.	Tagalog	24,516	1.1
10.	Russian	21,903	0.9
11.	Creole (French)	21,850	0.9
12.	Arabic	20,318	0.9
13.	Portugese	15,298	0.7
14.	Japanese	13,913	0.6
15.	Armenian	11,916	0.5
16.	Chinese (unspec.)	11,540	0.5
17.	Mandarin	11,020	0.5
18.	Farsi	8,563	0.4
19.	Hindi	7,905	0.3
20.	Polish	6,747	0.3

having the greatest numbers and the greatest variety of languages. Suburban and rural districts also have been impacted by other language speakers and by 1999 even regions that had not had other language speakers since the European immigrants were beginning to see significant numbers enrolling in schools. By 2001, Hispanic immigrants represented between 6 percent and 25 percent of the total population in counties in North Carolina, Georgia, Iowa, Arkansas, Minnesota, and Nebraska (U. S. Census, 1990). This was due to an increase of immigrant labor in farms, manufacturing, and other industries in these areas. Before, only certain geographic regions of the country needed to address educating children from non-English backgrounds. Now this need is widespread.

Status of Spanish in the United States

In spite of the political debate and controversy over Spanish, or maybe because of it, Spanish is the most widely studied foreign language in American elementary and secondary schools. It has a unique place in the linguistic history of our country. As we just discussed, it is the first European language firmly planted in what is now the United States. The Spanish colonization of the Southwest in the early sixteenth and seventeenth centuries was permanent. It was not, as commonly represented in American history books, conquistadores passing through naming places and then going back to Spain. We also share a border with a Spanish speaking country. This means that, as in all the rest of the world, there is an area along the border that is bilingual and bicultural, where trade and economic necessity make Spanish an advantageous language to know. Spanish is also unique in the United States in that it is the language of the historic enemy of the English speaking world. Spain and England were bitter rivals throughout the colonization period and some historians believe that the U.S. Anglo power structure inherited the animosity toward Spain. In the expansion of the United States, this built in bias manifested itself in discrimination toward Spanish speakers who were absorbed into the American society as a result of the treaties that ended the Spanish American War (Puerto Rico) in 1898 and the war with Mexico in 1848. As the West was settled, writers for the Eastern press often characterized Spanish speakers as lazy, treacherous, cruel, and cowardly (Sanchez, 1990), stereotypes that still permeate American media and the public school curriculum. Most Americans have been raised and were schooled with curriculum that either ignored the Spanish colonization of what is now the United States or described any contact with Spanish speaking populations in a perjorative manner.

Varieties of Spanish

Just as in English or any major language, there are varieties of Spanish that classroom teachers need to be aware of. Americans, British, Australians, and Canadians have their own dialects and distinctive ways of using English, as do Spanish speakers who have their own distinctive way of speaking Spanish, depending on national origin. Even within groups there are variations depending on what part of a country people come from and their educational backgrounds. For example, the Spanish used by Mexicans from southern Mexico can be distinguished from those in northern Mexico. It is worth noting here that children from isolated rural parts of Mexico may not even speak Spanish. Their native language may be the indigenous Indian language and Spanish may be a second language they are in the process of learning. This is also the case with some immigrants from Guatemala and other Central American countries. Educators can't assume that all immigrants from Latin America will be Spanish speakers, or that they will be proficient in Spanish.

Time spent in the United States and geographic region also determine the variety of Spanish people speak. For example, in the very isolated areas of northern New Mexico, the variety of Spanish used for centuries was much like the Spanish of the sixteenth and seventeenth centuries and is considered "old fashioned" by other Spanish speakers. On the other hand, Spanish used in cities like Miami and Los Angeles reflect modern Spanish that evolved in Cuba and Mexico respectively.

English in the Hispanic Community

As happens when linguistic communities coexist, Spanish and English have influenced each other in the United States. Many Spanish words incorporated into English demonstrate that Spanish has influenced American English vocabulary significantly, perhaps more than any other language. An example is the vocabulary associated with the ranching industry and cowboys. This is almost completely evolved from Spanish. Spanish words like *plaza*, *rodeo*, *patio*, and *ranch* are all words that have been incorporated into the American English vocabulary. English has also influenced Spanish as it is spoken within the United States. For example, in the Southwest, the word *troka* is commonly used for truck although the "real" Spanish word in dictionaries is *camión*.

Hispanic citizens value English and many have a strong desire to learn English. English is the official language of government as well and the language of upward mobility in American society. In general, Hispanics also value their heritage language and consequently are the most bilingual populations in the United States.

Bilingual Education and English as a Second Language Programs

Identification for Programs

Only children who are identified as being "limited English proficient" (LEP) are placed in bilingual or ESL programs. The word "limited" is used when children receive a particular score, usually below 3 on a scale of 1–5, on a measure of English proficiency. However, the tests that are used to determine whether students are LEP, are mostly measures of listening skills and to a lesser extent, speaking skills, so children don't have to be really proficient to get scores above 3. Certainly, it is possible for children to "test out" of bilingual/ESL programs and yet not have the necessary level of English to succeed in English only classrooms with no native language support in subject areas. The result is that many children who are still learning English are placed in regular, *non*-bilingual classrooms even though they may not be ready. This means that *all* classroom teachers, not only bilingual and

ESL teachers, are teaching children who are in the process of learning a second language. Most teachers can expect to have second language learners in their classrooms. In fact, even some children who are identified as needing bilingual and ESL programs are not in those programs because there are not enough programs to fill the need. In some cases, parents choose not to have their children in bilingual programs because they worry they won't learn English. There are even instances where teachers and administrators advise parents not to put their children in bilingual classrooms, not realizing that English as a Second Language is a critical component of bilingual programs. Some people estimate that over half of the children identified as eligible for bilingual or ESL programs are not in them.

The implications for teacher education are clear—all teachers should have some preparation for teaching children from non-English backgrounds. All teachers in American schools know English and we believe they can learn how to teach English as a Second Language to language minority students in their classrooms, including those Hispanic children who are learning English as a Second Language. The following gives some basic information about bilingual/ESL programs, principles, and practice in second language learning. Beyond knowing more about strategies for teaching ESL, all teachers have a professional obligation to understand the political context surrounding their Hispanic students who are literally caught in the middle of the bigger political debate over language use in public schools.

Historical Perspective on Bilingual and ESL Programs

Several factors promoted the establishment of modern bilingual programs in public schools. Refugees fleeing the Cuban Revolution in the late 1950s and 1960s brought an educated middle class with experienced teachers to the United States. They helped develop a bilingual program for Cuban *and* American children at the Coral Way Elementary School in Dade County, Florida. The program was in a public school but utilized funding from the Ford Foundation and was so successful in teaching Spanish and English speakers that it demonstrated bilingual instruction could be done to the benefit of everyone. This program spurred the development of other programs in other parts of the country where poorer, less educated Hispanic populations had long been demanding bilingual instruction with little success. Hispanic groups began to push for bilingual programs and their increasing political influence helped the passage of the federal Bilingual Education Act of 1968. Throughout the 1970s, federal and state legislation produced guidelines for programs, funding for teacher training, materials and curriculum development, and a variety of mechanisms for monitoring and evaluating programs.

The Civil Rights movement during the 1960s and 1970s was also instrumental in the proliferation of bilingual programs as it brought attention to inequities in schooling of ethnic and language minority students. Many court cases throughout the 1970s and 1980s mandated that school districts develop effective programs for children learning English as a Second Language. The courts did not generally prescribe what types of programs, only that districts demonstrate that programs were based on effective principles and practices.

By 1983 all 50 states had passed laws permitting and promoting bilingual education. By 1991 state legislatures were beginning to shift toward passing English only laws. A number of the laws, including Arizona's and Colorado's were deemed unconstitutional just after they passed, but in 1997 California, which has the largest numbers of limited English proficient students passed Proposition 227 which severely limited the number of years children could be in a bilingual program and required parents to request that their children be in bilingual programs. In 2000, Arizona also passed Proposition 203, which severely limited bilingual programs.

Bilingual programs are intended to teach English and to use the child's native language to teach subject areas like mathematics, science, and social studies, and to develop literacy. The programs are usually categorized and described as *transitional* or *developmental* depending on whether the programs' goal is to "transition" students into English-only classrooms as quickly as possible or to "develop" both the native language of students and English, that is to have students become bilingual. The majority of programs in the United States are transitional, with their main goal being to get students to a minimum proficiency in English and then transition them to mainstream English-only classrooms. Transitional programs use the children's native language, as needed, to teach subject areas but their focus is on getting children proficient enough to "exit" by getting a sufficiently high score on a language assessment test. Developmental programs, on the other hand, aspire to develop both English and the native language of the children so that they do become bilingual. Some developmental programs are called Two Way or Dual Language programs, because they include both English speakers and Spanish speakers and their goal is to develop bilingualism in *both* Spanish speakers and English speakers.

Identification for Bilingual or ESL Programs

When children enroll in public schools they are generally asked if there is a language other than English spoken at home. If the answer is yes, they are given some type of language assessment to determine if they need to be in bilingual or ESL programs. The assessment usually measures understanding of English and to some extent, the ability to speak English. Some common measures used are the Language Assessment Scale (LAS) and Language Assessment Battery (LAB). In some rare cases, students' native language proficiency is also assessed. If students receive scores below a certain cutoff on the English tests, they are determined to be limited English proficient or LEP. Federal and state legislation generally mandates programs for those least proficient, and schools are supposed to assign them to a particular program. Many bilingual and ESL educators dislike the negative aspect of the term "limited" and prefer to use English language learners (ELLS).

Only about 32 percent of school districts in the United States have bilingual or ESL programs and some estimate that as many as half of the children identified for these programs are actually in regular, mainstream classrooms taught by teachers who have not been prepared for them. According to federal guidelines, schools are supposed to provide bilingual programs when there are at least ten students identified from one language group at a grade level. Bilingual elementary schools generally have at least one classroom per grade level designated as bilingual classrooms and teachers who have been certified in elementary bilingual education are supposed to be assigned to these classrooms. Secondary schools in districts with large numbers of LEP students sometimes have bilingual classes for content areas like mathematics, science, and social studies as well as English as a Second Language classes.

Because bilingual programs are used when there is a critical mass of students, most programs are Spanish/English, Chinese/English, Vietnamese/English. However, districts usually have children from many different language groups, sometimes with only a few speakers of a language, so they are not always able to provide bilingual programs or teachers for children from all language backgrounds. Instead, children not in bilingual programs are assigned to English as a Second Language programs which are usually pull-out programs where the ESL teacher "pulls" children out of their regular classrooms for intensive English language instruction for anywhere from one to three hours per day. ESL teachers teach many different language groups at any given time and generally teach *only* English, not content areas. Ideally, they try to coordinate ESL with content area instruction in regular classrooms whenever possible.

In terms of teacher preparation for bilingual and ESL programs, there are differences in certification for bilingual and ESL teachers. ESL teaching requires certification in that area only. Bilingual teachers, however, are regular classroom teachers and are certified as elementary or secondary teachers. Secondary bilingual teachers are also required to have certification in their subject area with the added endorsement for bilingual education. Getting bilingual certification usually requires 18–21 credit hours beyond elementary or secondary certification.

In all school districts, the curriculum in bilingual classrooms is the same as for non-bilingual classrooms except for classes in ESL. Children are supposed to receive the same content instruction and to develop literacy in English. In developmental programs, all children are supposed to learn English and Spanish or any other language as well. The focus on language development is paramount—both bilingual and ESL teachers use methods and strategies to develop a second language. Classroom practice, including assessment of language and teaching of language that can be done in any classroom, bilingual or not, will be addressed in the next chapter.

EXERCISES FOR REFLECTION

Reflecting on Your Own Language Skills

1. Do you understand/speak/read/write a language other than English? If so, how did you learn that language? How proficient are you? Describe what you can do in another language. Compare that to what you can do in English.
2. Did you come from a family where a language other than English was used? Do any of your relatives understand/speak a language other than English?
3. Write a linguistic autobiography, describing how you learned your native language and a second language if applicable.
4. Did you take a foreign language in school? What was that like? Did you really learn how to communicate in that language? Have you had an opportunity to use that language in real life settings?

Reflecting on Language History in Our Country

1. Why did some languages of European immigrants die out in the United States?
2. What are your perceptions of French? Of German? Of Japanese?
3. Compare your perceptions of Spanish with your perceptions of French.

REFERENCES

Andersson, T., & Boyer, M. (1978). *Bilingual schooling in the U.S.* Austin, TX: National Educational Laboratory Publishers, Inc.

Castellanos, D. (1985). *The best of two worlds: Bilingual-bicultural education in the U.S.* Trenton, NJ: New Jersey State Department of Education.

Crawford, J. (1989). *Bilingual education: History, theory, and practice.* Trenton, NJ: Crane Publishing Company, Inc.
Sanchez, J. P. (1990). *The Spanish black legend: Origins of anti-Hispanic stereotypes.* Series No. 2. Albuquerque, NM: Spanish Colonial Research Center, University of New Mexico.
San Miguel, G., & Valencia, R. (1998). From the Treaty of Guadalupe Hidalgo to Hopwood: The educational plight and struggle of Mexican Americans in the Southwest. *Harvard Educational Review, 68*(3), 353–410.
U.S. Census. (1990). Washington, DC: U.S. Department of Commerce.

CHAPTER

5 Implications of Language Differences for the Classroom

This chapter covers the following topics:

- Issues related to language assessment
- Assessing language dominance and proficiency
- Formal and informal assessments
- Receptive and expressive aspects of language
- Listening, speaking, reading, and writing
- Vocabulary
- Language teaching
- Bilingual development
- Language development for everyone
- Integrating language and content areas

Because of the importance of language in the education of Hispanic students, this chapter will deal with basic ideas that classroom teachers need to know when they have children who are bilingual or learning English as a Second Language in their classrooms. Teachers need to be able to assess and develop language skills in either English, Spanish, or both. Since there are so many excellent resources on strategies for assessing and teaching in bilingual contexts already available, this chapter does not go into depth on those topics. Rather, the chapter gives an overview of important considerations in teaching Hispanic children and references are given for more reading and classroom assessment measures and instructional strategies.

In teaching all children, but especially in teaching children who have two languages in their life's experience, teachers must be able to accurately assess where children are in their development of all-important language skills so necessary for academic success. Having done valid and appropriate assessments, they will be able to effectively plan instruction that develops language and cognition.

Language Assessment

Definition of Terms

Before teachers can begin to plan lessons for developing language skills they must understand what skills students already have. The first thing to do is to assess Hispanic students' language dominance and language proficiency. *Dominance* refers to which language is stronger for a child. Children may be able to use two languages, but one will likely be stronger than the other and they will feel more comfortable using it for most purposes. The dominant language for most people is their first or native language. In the case of Hispanic children in the United States, the dominant or stronger language can be English or Spanish.

Proficiency refers to how well a child can use any given language. We can think of it as the "level" students are at in their control of language—in the broadest terms, beginning, intermediate, or advanced. Children may be fluent in two languages, in other words have proficiency in two languages, or they may be very proficient in one, and just beginning in another. To adequately develop Hispanic children's language skills, teachers need to understand the concepts of dominance and proficiency because most Hispanic students have had some experience with two languages, Spanish and English. In most cases the experience is stronger with one of the languages. Very few have had the opportunity to live in a completely balanced bilingual world. For most Hispanic children, their family experience will include Spanish, even though some children may not be really proficient in the use of Spanish. On the other hand, for most Hispanic children their school experience will be predominantly in English so they will have mixed levels of proficiency in each language.

Before discussing language proficiency and dominance any further, it is helpful to define the term *bilingual.* The word is often misused, resulting in misunderstanding and inappropriate labeling of children. *Bi* means two and *lingual* means having to do with language, so it basically means that a bilingual person makes use of two languages. There are relatively few truly balanced bilingual people with equal proficiency in two languages. People are generally stronger in one language or another, even though they can function effectively using both. For example, people growing up in a home where Spanish is the main language might have received all of their education in English. They may be very fluent in *speaking* Spanish, but not very good at *writing* in Spanish. In the United States, the term bilingual is often used to refer to Hispanic populations but in fact, it should be used to refer to any people who have proficiency in any two languages, not to a specific ethnic group. Many Asian Americans, Native Americans, and European Americans also use two languages and are bilingual.

Assessing Language Dominance and Proficiency

Language use varies a great deal within Hispanic populations, even within each Hispanic subgroup. The language used depends on where people were born and on how long they have lived in this country. In some parts of the country where there are large numbers of Hispanic people who speak Spanish, for example, along the U.S.–Mexico border, a high percentage of children will generally be fluent in Spanish as they enter school. Their knowledge of English will depend on how much contact they have had with English speaking peers or adults. This contact with English speakers often is related to parents' jobs and socioeconomic status and education. Children living in poorer, segregated neighborhoods may have learned English from television or older siblings, but they may not have had much reason to use English until they enter school—even if they were born in this country—because they have only had contact with Spanish speaking populations. On the other hand, Hispanic children born in this country and living in middle class integrated neighborhoods will have had much more contact with English speakers and will not only have a better understanding of English, they will have more opportunity to speak it. Their parents are also much more likely to be bilingual.

The trend is that as Hispanic children enter school, English begins to play a much bigger role in their lives. This point of entry to school for Hispanic children is often the determiner of academic success. Judgements made by school personnel about Hispanic children's language dominance and proficiency at this point largely determine their success. In most school districts, children who come from homes where a language other than English is spoken will be assessed to determine whether they should be in bilingual or ESL programs. If they are judged to be "English proficient," they are placed in regular, non-bilingual classrooms. Unfortunately, with few exceptions, the assessments made are not in depth, only measuring listening and sometimes speaking skills. They generally only measure English proficiency and ignore a child's proficiency in his dominant language. There are many Hispanic children who understand and speak English well enough to make a "passing" score on these measurements, but because their native language is Spanish, their score is not likely to reflect all that they know about using a language. Further, their score will place them in English-only classrooms where they will be expected to compete with native English speakers. When they are not all able to—they don't have the same level of proficiency as native speakers—they may be judged as disadvantaged or "behind" in knowledge as well as language. This tragically begins their path to failure, when realistically, the inappropriate assessment is what failed the children.

Children that come from Spanish speaking or bilingual (Spanish and English) homes and are being raised in an English speaking country, have contact with both languages. That contact and subsequent knowledge is mixed. Children will have strengths and weaknesses in both. They may be fluent *speakers* of Spanish, but have not had the chance to *read* in Spanish. They may understand English fairly well, but not be able to speak it fluently or to write in English.

Bilingual Development

Geographic location also makes a big difference in how and whether children will develop bilingually. Living in regions where Spanish speaking communities are in the minority limits children's contact with Spanish to their immediate families and neighborhoods. This lessens their chances of growing up bilingually. On the other hand, in states like Texas, California, Arizona, New Mexico, and Florida where Spanish has been a major language for centuries and where Hispanic immigration continues to keep the language vibrant, large communities are bilingual and children growing up there have every opportunity to develop both of their languages. For example, along the Mexican border and in Florida, especially Miami, where large numbers of Cuban refugees settled in the late 1950s and 1960s, the community itself is bilingual. Spanish is a common home language and is used along with English in everyday commerce and social interaction within the larger community. In other parts of the country, however, like the South or upper Midwest, Hispanic communities are smaller and more isolated. These communities are less likely to be bilingual. The context of schooling for Hispanic children and the available resources are markedly different depending on the region and on the size of the Hispanic community itself.

Finally, even though most Hispanic children have some knowledge of Spanish, we can't assume that they all speak or understand Spanish. If they are second generation or more, especially if they live in a region that is not bilingual and bicultural, they are very likely to be dominant English speakers, even exclusively English speaking. Their native language is English. If grandparents are the only ones who speak Spanish in the family, many

Hispanic children grow up with a receptive knowledge of Spanish, but have difficulty in producing it. Even when Hispanic students have some proficiency in Spanish as they enter elementary school, when that language is not developed in school, they eventually lose their ability to use Spanish and become monolingual English speakers. When any language skills are not used and developed, they are lost.

Consequences of Inadequate Assessment

Accurate, effective assessment of language for Hispanic students is vital to their success in school and cannot be overemphasized. Misunderstanding students' dominance and proficiency in their native language and second language not only limits the expectations for students in regular classrooms, it often results in misplacement into special education programs. On the other hand, sometimes children who do need special education services do not receive them because educators think the child's problem is only that he is learning English. According to Paredes Scribner (1999, p. 185), language assessment "should examine the way in which students process language to determine specific situations in which they perform as expected and others where they demonstrate difficulty." This sums up the purposes of assessment, and if looked at in this way, schools should use multiple measures, such as observations of children with peers as well as with teachers, language use questionnaires, culturally appropriate narratives, and spontaneous oral and written language samples, and standardized and teacher made tests. Performance-based assessments which include student work samples, such as portfolios or any collection of children's work, can be used by teachers to get a good picture of children's language dominance and proficiency.

Formal Assessments

Hispanic children who are in non-bilingual classrooms (and this is the majority of Hispanic students) take all the same tests and assessments that are required of all children. Because the tests are generally standardized tests, they may be culturally inappropriate for Hispanic children, even those who are born in this country. The tests are generally normed on mainstream, white middle class populations. Many Hispanic children live in neighborhoods that tend to be segregated and apart from the mainstream. Even when some Hispanics are included in the norming sample they still may be culturally inappropriate. For example, tests normed on Mexican American populations in California, are inappropriate for Puerto Rican children or even for other Mexican Americans in rural Arizona.

Spanish-speaking children in bilingual programs in larger school districts with comprehensive bilingual programs may take standardized tests in Spanish or English, sometimes in both. Otherwise, speakers of languages other than English usually do not take standardized tests or other formal measures until they reach a certain level of proficiency in English. The most widely used formal assessments are standardized achievement tests, mostly in English, but there are a few Spanish standardized tests used in large districts. Some of the most commonly used in English are the Stanford Nine, Iowa Test of Basic Skills, and in Spanish, the Aprenda. These and other tests are sometimes used to screen or do further assessments for Special Education and Gifted and Talented programs.

Informal Assessments for Classrooms

From the first day of school, teachers can begin evaluating students' language proficiency and dominance informally through the use of multiple, authentic performance measures such as portfolios, projects, or any collection of students' work over a period of time. Teachers may decide to collect key pieces of required work in a child's native language or both languages to evaluate before going on to other skills or curriculum, or they may select important pieces of work produced by students whenever they see something that indicates mastery of a skill or progress. Keeping folders of students' work over a period of time will demonstrate growth or lack of it, and will demonstrate specific skills that are mastered or not. Children should be allowed and encouraged to select their own work to include in portfolios, folders, displays, or any collection of their language products. These collections should include not only writing samples, but evidence of materials read, transcripts of oral samples, or the tapes themselves. They can also include art work that shows interpretations of what was said or read to children or that help interpret children's thinking.

Stop, Look, and Listen—for Both Languages

To assess both languages in the classrooms, students must have the opportunity to show what they can do, how well they can listen, speak, read, and write in both languages—without forcing them to perform in either one. In most cases, students will choose the language they are most comfortable with, and that alone will give the teacher some idea of which language is the child's dominant language. Sometimes, though, even if children are dominant in Spanish, they will choose to perform in English to demonstrate that they can use English. This may be because Spanish is discouraged in schools and has less status in American society or just that students want to belong by using the majority language. In any case, children and their choice in language should not be negated, but they should be encouraged to do both if they can. This will give the teacher an opportunity to *compare proficiency in both languages* and make informed decisions about what they need to teach in each language. For example, if a teacher collects writing in both languages and sees that a child:

- Writes complete sentences using sophisticated vocabulary in Spanish
- Correctly uses English syntax although writes short, choppy sentences
- Uses very limited vocabulary in English

the teacher then knows:

- The child is dominant in Spanish
- The child is "good" in the use of his native language
- The child has learned the structure of English sentences
- Needs work on English vocabulary
- The child should not be labeled as slow, or worse, that the child doesn't have language skills

Another important thing the teacher can see is that the child may have difficulty understanding lessons in mathematics, science, and social studies when taught in English, even though there is nothing "wrong" with him/her. The child just has not heard, and therefore not learned, the vocabulary necessary to completely grasp the subject lessons in English.

Then Act! What to Do

There are several things the teacher can do in a case like the one above. One, the teacher can reteach and check on comprehension of content lessons in Spanish. If the teacher cannot teach in Spanish, the teacher should preview the lesson, looking for English vocabulary words that are *key* to the lesson and then identify words that are likely to be new to a child learning ESL (probably words not in everyday conversation). Teaching the English words to Spanish dominant students *before* the actual lesson will help pave the way for learning concepts. The English vocabulary that may be new to children from Spanish home backgrounds may already be known by native English speaking peers, but sometimes teachers would do well to do "vocabulary checks" before teaching any lesson to all children, as many children are in need of vocabulary development. Sometimes English speakers may not know specialized English vocabulary for certain subjects. Making side-by-side lists of key words in Spanish and English can help fill in gaps for speakers of either language and promote bilingual development for all.

Receptive and Expressive Aspects of Language

As babies learn their native language, they receive input from speakers of that language, usually their parents and primary caretakers, which provides what they need in order to make sense out of the sounds and patterns of words they hear. They learn, first to listen, then to try to produce the sounds and combinations of sounds that have meaning to those around them. When babies successfully transmit their messages, they receive positive reinforcement and encouragement which stimulates them to continue trying.

Listening is a receptive area of language and speaking is an expressive or productive area. Later, as children learn to read and write, they learn that print is part of their linguistic code, that they receive linguistic input through reading, and that they can produce the print themselves to communicate meaning.

At any given time, children may be more proficient in receiving meaning through linguistic *input* (listening, reading) than in producing meaningful (speaking, writing) *output.* Young children understand the long sentences and talk of adults, but can only use shortcut sentences or "baby talk" when they talk to others. Even though they understand the longer, complex sentences produced by adults, they themselves can't yet produce them. Common "errors" children make, like saying "foots" instead of feet, demonstrate that children are figuring out their linguistic code. They understand the difference between singular and plural because they know that the rule in English is to add an "s" to words to indicate more than one thing. However, in producing words, they are still learning the exceptions to the rule—but, they have figured out the rule.

The pattern of language learning is that learners are better at receiving messages than they are at producing for a while. This is important to remember when dealing with children who are learning a second language. They are sometimes able to understand, but are at a loss to speak, at least to fluently express what they do understand. Therefore, it is important for teachers to be able to assess what children are *understanding*, even before they judge what children are producing.

It is difficult to assess children with more than one language in their background because they may be at different levels in their receptive skills in their native language *and* will almost certainly be at different levels in producing their second language as they enter school. Without close attention to developing both languages, they will most certainly remain at different levels or even lose skills, particularly expressive skills in one or the other. It is common to find Hispanic adults who were dominant Spanish speakers as they entered school, but because only English was developed in school, they lost the ability to produce Spanish. Yet, they usually retain their receptive ability and do understand Spanish well. Because of this complexity and the difficulty of separating the receptive and expressive aspects of language, we will consider listening, speaking, reading, and writing together although teachers should provide opportunities for focusing on assessing and teaching each area specifically.

Assessing Listening, Speaking, Reading, and Writing Skills

Listening is basically a skill of cognitive attention to what someone is saying, to sounds and sound patterns, assuming no hearing loss on the part of the listener. This is a neglected area in elementary and secondary schools in terms of evaluation and instruction. Students at secondary level are expected to have good listening skills since so much of the teaching is done orally in high schools, but this isn't an area that receives much focus except in kindergarten. For children learning a second language, it is a critical area because if they don't receive comprehensible input to listen to, they cannot learn how to say anything in a second language. They must hear the new language and hear it consistently in order to make sense out of it. This is especially true for young children who have not yet learned how to read. Older students may have reading and writing skills they can use to help them learn a new language but young children have to rely on what they hear.

Professional Reflection

When trying to figure out what Spanish speaking children know in English, observe how they react to what you say and listen to what they say to you. If a child didn't seem to understand you, did he/she just not recognize the sounds well enough to make out words or did they just not know the meaning of the word? Did the child repeat a word, but not know what it meant? If it is a matter of sounds, then the instruction the teacher needs to provide is more opportunity to listen to English words, especially English spoken in a normal steady stream instead of in isolation in word lists. If the assessment was that the child heard the word and repeated it, but that he/she didn't know what it meant, then it is a matter of explaining the meaning. Depending on the assessment, the follow-up lesson will deal with phonetic structure of English or with semantics (meaning of words).

Evaluating a child's listening skills can be difficult because it requires that teachers pay attention to each individual, and listening to each child requires a great deal of planning. Teachers need to look for every minute available to talk with individuals and note what children say to them. This can be done in small or large groups as well as individually, but if the exercises are done in English and children are unsure of speaking English, they are not likely to volunteer—even if they think they have understood. When teachers check understanding by questioning the entire class, individuals who are operating in a second language or limited English skills may drop through the cracks. This makes it necessary to find ways of individualizing the assessment, to see exactly where gaps are.

Teachers have to make use of any language produced by students at any time, not just when its time to test. The following language sample, written by a fourth grader learning ESL, can tell us something about the listening, speaking, writing, and to some extent, reading skills of the child. Children were asked to write about their Halloween plans. Let's evaluate the sample by reading this piece of writing printed below just as it was written by the child.

> Tonight I am going to Halloween because I want a sker the prseins because I am kana be a witch and I am ruilly happy because is Halloween and I wan a inbait o my friends to my house and to get candys wet o my friends and I wan to go to get candys wet o my friends because I laike o my friends and I laike o my friends and dats o. Happy Halloween.

Can you understand what this child wanted to say? Even though there are errors in spelling and the paragraph is one long sentence, we can still understand what the student means. Now, instead of marking the student down for spelling words incorrectly and using a sentence that is too long, lets see what the language sample can tell us about the English listening, speaking, writing, and reading skills of this child.

Lets Practice Together

First, can you tell that this was written by someone learning English as a Second Language? How? One clue is in the way the child phrased things, for example, *I am going to Halloween.* We know the child is going to participate in Halloween activities, but a native speaker of English would not say he is *going to* Halloween. Other clues are in the way words are spelled. Look at *sker*, *inbait*, *laike*, and *ruilly*. You can probably see that if you pronounce these words the way the child spelled them, you will sound like you have a Spanish accent. The vowels in Spanish always have the same sound—*a* is pronounced like *ah*, *e* is *eh*, *i* is like long *e* in English, *u* is *oo* like in *boo*. Say *sker*, *inbait* (*ah* + long *e* in English), *laike* (*ah* + long *e* in English), and *ruilly* (*oo* + long *e*) out loud and hear how they sound. The consonants *b* and *v* are very similar in Spanish and even Spanish speakers have a difficult time hearing the difference

The child does know how to use and spell many English words, even words like *tonight*, *because*, *witch*, and *Halloween*. These are not easy words to spell, even for English speakers, because they are not spelled like they sound. This indicates that the student learned them in class, probably in spelling lessons (I'll bet they were on the week's spelling list). But, other words that are consistently misspelled give clues that this child is spelling words the way they sound in Spanish. Native English speakers might make some of the same spelling errors, but if they spelled the more difficult words like *because* and *tonight* correctly, they probably would also have spelled the more common words (not necessarily easier) like *really*, *invite*, and *like* correctly. The writer of this Halloween paragraph might not have had the chance to learn the other, more common words that native English speakers would already probably know. However, ESL classes are having some success. Note that the child has learned that there is a silent *e* at the end of *like* and that there is a *y* at the end of *really* so the child has learned some "rules" about English spelling. The harder part is always the vowel sounds in the middle of words.

Looking at this language sample then, tells us something about the listening and speaking proficiency of this child in English. The child actually knows a lot of words in English and aside from the long sentence, seems to understand the order of words in English as well. It is important for teachers to give ESL students opportunities to write and talk because teachers may not pick up on how children are hearing English words just by listening to them. They would understand the child and think the child just has an accent.

Implications for Planning Instruction

In this case, because the child consistently uses *a* instead of *to* and leaves off the ending *t* in *want*, as in "I wan a" the teacher should make sure to clearly pronounce the *t* when saying "want to" and show the spelling of the words when saying them so the child sees and hears *t* in *want* and in *to*. The teacher also has to provide many opportunities for Spanish speakers to hear vowels and see the spellings of words using the different vowel sounds in English. Since there is such a precise and consistent letter-sound correspondence for vowels in Spanish, all the variations and exceptions for vowel sounds in English are confusing for Spanish speakers, in fact, they are confusing for all who are learning ESL, no matter what their native language is.

In the case of the child who wrote the sample above, we can learn something about the child's reading skills by having the child read this sample. Observing children read is a most effective way of assessing reading skills, both in sounding out words and in comprehension. Having the child read his statement out loud would help the teacher know how the child produces the English words (which is directly connected to how he/she hears the words). Taking notes on the child's reading behaviors (strategies for sounding out words, for example) for later reference will help teachers plan for specific instructional needs of individuals. It is very important to check for comprehension when children read in their second language as well as listening to how they pronounce words. Children often "fool" teachers when they are able to sound out words, but they may have no idea what they mean. All they need then, is an explanation of the meaning of the word.

In terms of teaching writing skills, this sample tells the teacher the child needs some modeling for writing sentences. The teacher could easily model breaking up the long sentence into shorter ones by writing back to the child, using the same words in shorter sentences.

Is there anything else we can learn from this language sample? We see that the child understands the American cultural celebration of Halloween. The child writes about asking for candy, gathering with friends, and scaring others as part of Halloween. Beyond clues about language skills and cultural knowledge, the sample may give indications about special needs. For example, there may be some things the teacher should check out based on this language sample. There are a number of words that indicate the child is not hearing some English sounds. Examples of these are *wan* for *want*, *kana* for *going to* (or *gonna*, which is common for English speakers to hear and write), *wet* for *with*, and *o* for *all*. Depending on how long this child has been in school listening to English, this may or may not indicate a hearing problem. If the child has been in the English classroom for a long time, the fact that he has so many sound/symbol "miscues" might suggest that his hearing should be tested. If he has not been in this country very long and is just beginning to learn English, this may not be anything more than difficulty distinguishing English sounds at this point.

Managing Classroom Assessment

Conversations. The most effective way to make sure you understand how well a child listened to anything is to ask questions and talk with the child about what he/she heard. This doesn't have to be extensive or require notetaking. Identifying key questions and casually asking in a conversational way quickly gives teachers information. This is sometimes difficult with a roomful of children needing the teacher's attention, but there are ways to organize yourself to do it. Putting children to work with each other or individually can provide short periods of time for teachers to talk with individuals. Keeping a checklist of skills you are looking for or keeping a running log to write notes about each child in a notebook allows you to quickly note your talk with each child and your assessment of what he/she is learning. This helps later to plan your lessons. Taping children's answers also allows evaluation at a later time.

Just talking with children kills many birds with one stone. Teachers can assess what a child understood in English and, if teachers are talking about mathematics, science, or social studies, they can evaluate what the child learned about any given subject as well as what they are learning about language. Taking the time to converse with children also addresses another factor found to be critical in teaching Hispanic children. That factor is that effective teachers of Hispanic children provide a nurturing environment where children are paid attention to and valued. The personal connection made by conversing with children is important in teaching all children, but according to research, it is critical in the schooling of most Hispanic students.

Observation. Another effective way of assessing listening and speaking skills is to observe the natural interaction between children when they are playing, working with each other in the classroom, or just talking in the hallway. Allowing opportunities for children to talk and listen to each other in classrooms not only gives children a chance to practice skills in English and their native language, it gives teachers something to assess. Peer interaction addresses another factor that has been documented as critical in teaching Hispanic children. Research indicates Hispanic families socialize children to learn from each other, to cooperate in the accomplishment of tasks, and to work toward the good of family, which in this case is the classroom (Valdez, 1996).

Focused Listening. Many American classrooms do not accept verbal interaction between students as a valid way of learning, exploring, and clarifying concepts. But, among peers, it is a most valuable way of learning. Recording interaction among children is a good way to collect information when the teacher is not able to listen to everyone at the same time. This can be done by having an assistant tape record discussions, conversations, or even having the children tape each other. Children can easily learn how to handle tape recorders and they are not cumbersome to have in various locations throughout the classrooms. If teachers want to assess something in particular, they may assign a topic to keep the discussion focused. Even young children can read a series of simply worded questions to each other. Games, riddles, and puzzles that require listening to directions or information are good ways of eliciting oral language skills that give information about how well children can understand and speak a language.

Vocabulary Assessment

Vocabulary knowledge, in particular, is a key indicator of proficiency in a language. However, just knowing words in isolation isn't always indicative of proficiency in using a language. Many of the formal and informal assessments on the market for ESL are basically tests of vocabulary knowledge. Because vocabulary is important and is often part of standardized tests, it is important that children know words commonly used in academic settings. Vocabulary assessments are also important in content area learning. Even when a child is dominant in Spanish, learning the English equivalent of words or concepts that he/she already knows enhances concepts and learning in content areas. Finally, learning vocabulary is relatively easy and can be fun for children learning a second language to do. There are hundreds of activities for children in reading and language arts texts and children's self-confidence can be boosted by learning new words daily. Making sure that you provide a vocabulary building exercise every day for all children, but specifically providing input for learning English as a second language is a very doable thing for teachers at all grade levels.

Language Teaching

Full-Scale Assault

When we look at research on effective teaching for Hispanic students we find that effective teachers spend a great deal of time and effort on facilitating language development—and they don't worry about which language a child uses to learn. They facilitate language development, and don't try to minimize one language or the other. They allow both of the children's languages to be developed and they plan time for developing both. Because of the complexity of Hispanic students' linguistic background, this emphasis on language development is crucial. Even those students who are deemed to be English proficient can have gaps that can only be filled by enhancing the students' educational experience with language, the more the better in both languages. Research on bilingualism conducted with many different combinations of languages demonstrates cognitive benefits to being bilingual, as well as social and economic benefits. It increases in the ability to think in alternate codes (Collier, 1995; Krashen & Biber, 1988). Teachers should not deny Hispanic children who already have the beginnings of two languages the potential benefits of bilingualism. In fact, the opportunity should be provided for *all* children in American schools to learn a second language and to have the benefits of being bilingual.

Language Teaching for Hispanic Monolingual English Speakers

As we discussed earlier in this textbook, Hispanic children do not always have strong skills in Spanish. So, just as we can't assume that Hispanic children know English just because they can understand and speak a few phrases, we also can't assume they know Spanish just because they can understand some. In fact, the majority of Hispanic children born in this country are dominant in English. An important thing to find out is whether students are afraid or ashamed to speak Spanish or really don't know it. Families may value Spanish, but the American society in general has not. Considering the laws and campaigns to ban it in public places, it should be no surprise that sometimes Hispanic children are ambivalent about using Spanish. On the other hand, if they were born here and haven't learned Spanish at home, they can be made to feel ashamed that they don't know Spanish if teachers expect that they *should* know Spanish.

Careful observations by teachers will help them know the relative strengths of a child's language. Observation and talking with children and parents can tell teachers that Hispanic children may have only one language, and in some cases, that language will be English. If a Hispanic child's native language is English, there may not be many adjustments to be made by the teacher. However, teachers who learn to be effective teachers of Hispanic children also learn to be strong language teachers. Their classroom teaching then automatically adjusts to improve language teaching for *all* children.

Language Development for Everyone

There are some classrooms where all children are Hispanic or constitute a good percentage of the entire class. In these cases, the teacher can incorporate a lot of language development into every day's curriculum (including mathematics, science, social studies), paying particular attention to second language learning. On the other hand, other classrooms have smaller percentages of Hispanic students in them. Does this mean the teacher has to plan differently for the Hispanic children? In a sense, yes, because the teacher has to address each child's needs. However, an emphasis on language development will benefit all children, including native speakers of English. Many Hispanic children attend schools that are in high poverty areas where all children, including native English speakers, need opportunities for language development. Helping all teachers to become better teachers of language will benefit not only Hispanic children from bilingual backgrounds, but all students. Promoting the use of Spanish (or any other language present in the student population) in the classroom can expose English speakers to the benefits of learning and recognizing other languages.

Professional Reflection

There are some excellent sources for ESL teaching strategies, but the following are particularly good for classroom teachers. Two extremely useful sources for teaching strategies are *Learning in Two Worlds*, by Bertha Perez and Maria Torres-Guzman and *Language Minority Students in the Mainstream Classroom*, by Angela Carrasquillo and Vivian Rodriguez. *Learning in Two Worlds* is an excellent source of information on the variety of Hispanic populations and their home and school contexts. It has a wealth of specific strategies and classroom suggestions to effectively develop the language skills of children growing up in a bilingual world. *Language Minority Students in the Mainstream Classroom* directly addresses the context and needs of classroom teachers who are not certified bilingual or ESL teachers. *Bilingual and ESL Classrooms: Teaching in Multicultural Contexts* by Carlos Ovando and Virginia Collier has some great sections on integrating language into mathematics, science, social studies, music, and art. A chapter in *Making Schooling Multicultural: Campus and Classroom* by Toni Griego Jones has a useful section on classroom organization and how to phase in learning of a second language.

Summary

It is possible for teachers who are *not* Hispanic and *not* bilingual to promote language, even bilingual development, in the classroom and to be very effective teachers of Hispanic children. The following suggestions for teaching strategies and approaches are for classrooms that are not part of bilingual programs, but that do have Hispanic children who are very likely at all stages of bilingual development. First, teachers must create an environment that facilitates and celebrates language development.

- Do not prohibit or discourage Spanish speakers from using their native language to learn about content areas or about how to read and write. The skills they develop in Spanish reading and writing automatically transfer to English as they learn more English.
- Encourage children to practice language (speaking, reading, writing) in either language, even if they are not yet able to express themselves perfectly.

- Make your classroom a place where they hear English spoken well and often.
- Be encouraging so they feel comfortable taking risks in trying out what they hear, and ensure they are not teased when they try.
- Honor both of their languages if they have two.

Second, highlight the contributions of Spanish to American English. This is good for all students, not just Hispanic children, because everyone should know about these contributions and understand how languages influence each other when they come together. This is the history of human language development. People influence each other's languages as they borrow words, phrases, and terms and incorporate them into their own languages. Looking at contact between speakers of different languages as a natural phenomenon can minimize the fear of other languages that seems to be so prevalent in American society.

Third, every American classroom teacher can be a teacher of English as a Second Language. Every teacher knows English and can teach it to native speakers and to those who are learning it as their second language. The bottom line for "regular" classroom teachers is that they are the English role models for children learning a second language. This means they have to make sure the "input" they are giving ESL students is comprehensible, that they structure their speaking so that children will understand them and learn the English words they are using. Teachers have to give numerous opportunities for children to hear English, to read it, and to practice speaking and writing. Think about it, how many times would you have to hear new words and phrases in a foreign language before you could understand them, replicate them, remember them, and say them in a natural way in sentences, and then write them in comprehensible ways? Learning a second language is not an easy task. It is every teacher's responsibility to thoughtfully plan instruction for his/her students who are in their classroom to learn English.

EXERCISES FOR REFLECTION

Reflect on your own language skills, how you learned them, and how you use them.

1. How well do you listen? What did a child tell you today? What was the first thing someone said to you today? What is hard about listening?

2. How do you feel speaking in front of a group of people? With friends? At a party? In conversations with friends or colleagues, do you use the same words over and over again? How do you organize what you are going to say—your thoughts—in speaking with friends? In a lesson with your students?

   What do you talk to your students about? Do you ever just talk with your students about non-academic subjects? Do you talk to each of them every day? How many did you just talk with today?

3. How did you learn to read? Did you like to read when you were a child? Do you like to read now? What was easy about learning to read? What was difficult?
4. Do you remember learning to write? How did it happen? Did you like to write in school? Do you like to now? How often do you write? What kinds of things do you write?
5. Look in an American dictionary and note how many words come from Latin, or from the romance languages—Spanish, French, Italian, Portuguese. How many Spanish words do you already know and use in everyday American speech?
6. Do you understand, speak, read, or write a language other than English? How did you learn this language? Have you ever been in a situation where you had to use this other language? Are you able to really use it when you have to communicate with a native speaker of that language? How did you feel when you had to use a language other than your native language?

REFERENCES

Carrasquillo, A. L., & Rodriguez, V. (1996). *Language minority students in the mainstream classroom.* Philadelphia: Multilingual Matters, Ltd.

Collier, V. (1995). *Promoting academic success for ESL students: Understanding second language acquisition for school.* Jersey City, NJ: NJTSOL-BE/Multicultural Center/Office of Publications and Special Programs at Jersey City State College.

Griego Jones, T. (1996). Reconstructing bilingual education from a multicultural perspective. In C. A. Grant & M. L. Gomez (Eds.), *Making schooling multicultural* (pp. 111–131). Englewood Cliffs, NJ: Merrill.

Krashen, S., & Biber, D. (1988). On course: Bilingual education's success in California. Sacramento: California Association for Bilingual Education.

Ovando, C. J., & Collier, V. P. (1985). *Bilingual and ESL classrooms: Teaching in multicultural contexts.* New York: McGraw Hill, Inc.

Paredes Scribner, A. (1999). Using student advocacy assessment practices. In P. Reyes, J. D. Scribner, & A. Paredes Scribner (Eds.), *Lessons from high-performing Hispanic schools* (pp. 169–187). New York: Teachers College Press.

Perez, B., & Torres-Guzman, M. (2002). *Learning in two worlds: An integrated Spanish/English biliteracy approach* (Rev. ed.). Boston: Allyn & Bacon.

Valdez, G. (1996). *Con respeto: Bridging the distance between culturally diverse families and schools: An ethnographic portrait.* New York: Teacher's College Press.

CHAPTER

6 Teaching Hispanic Students

This chapter covers the following topics:

- Cultural sensitivity and cultural diversity
- Socioeconomic factors
- Classroom expectations
- Equity and effective teaching
- Factors influencing Hispanic children's learning
- Cultural traits
- Stereotypes
- Classroom implications

Too often we as educators look for "the answer" to teaching students—in this case Hispanic students. We look for the formula (the one size fits all approach) that will result in the perfect educational strategy that will fill the needs of all students. Unfortunately, for such a formula to work, all ingredients must be identical. However, when dealing with people, there is too much variability between individuals and groups for a single plan of action. We much be knowledgeable about and appreciate the variety of factors which make individuals unique.

Information about families, economics, communities, cultural background, and so on can help you develop a basic understanding of your students. The purpose of this chapter is to provide information that will help you better understand, appreciate, and teach Hispanic children.

Historically the school system in this country has often ignored and stereotyped Mexican students. The segregation of Hispanic students was not as blatant as it was for African American students but it was a reality nevertheless. There were schools in Arizona, New Mexico, Texas, and California that at one time maintained segregated schools or classrooms for Mexican Americans. Not until 1970, 16 years after the Supreme Court's

Brown decision declared racially segregated schools unconstitutional, did a Texas district court judge rule in *Cisneros v. Corpus Christi* that Mexican Americans should be treated as an identifiable minority group, and that the combination of two minority groups apart from white, non Hispanic students did not achieve desegregation (Valdez, 1996).

What has happened in those intervening years? Hispanic students have had little access to quality education programs, a higher percent of school retention than white, non-Hispanic students, and a much higher dropout rate. They also use a curriculum that doesn't recognize them or the accomplishments of their culture, and the Hispanic student is more apt to be placed in a special education setting than their white mainstream counterparts (Carrasquillo, 1991).

Obviously, the education of Hispanic groups needs to change dramatically. This is neither an easy or inexpensive task, however, justice demands equity in education. This chapter covers classroom issues for teachers. However, it is the responsibility of all of society, not just educators, to see that all children attend quality schools, have well prepared teachers, have the resources needed for children to learn, and facilities that make school a safe and pleasant place to be.

Cultural Sensitivity

Cultural sensitivity—that is, being able to recognize, appreciate, and understand cultures other than your own—is a prerequisite for good teaching. Cultural sensitivity requires that teachers have an idea of what *a culture* is generally and what *their culture* (the teacher's culture) looks like specifically. Too often Euro-American educators don't recognize their own culture and so feel that culture is limited to exotic people living elsewhere. These teachers do not recognize that they are deeply rooted in their own cultures, and that their culture is the source of their values, their behaviors, and their perspectives on their lives and the world in which they live. Glazer and Moynihan note that even after four or five generations, people are still influenced by their ancestors' cultures even though they may have limited knowledge of those cultures (1991).

Knowledge of one's own culture guides teachers' relationships with their students. Teachers who lack cultural sensitivity interpret their students' values and behaviors, for example, in light of their own cultural norms—with the result that children from diverse populations often come up lacking. By not recognizing their students' cultures, teachers communicate an unacceptable message to their students; the teachers deny the students' cultures worth or, even worse, the cultures' existence. It is easy for culturally insensitive teachers to fall into the trap of being ethnocentric (i.e., assuming that their culture is right and that cultures doing things differently are automatically wrong), and so make ethnocentric judgments that hinder communication. At worst, such judgments causes irreparable harm to the relationships teachers are working to establish with their Hispanic students.

Those educators who are culturally relative (i.e., possessing the ability to view other cultures in nonjudgmental ways) can recognize and appreciate both their own culture and the cultures of others. This allows those teachers to examine the characteristics of Hispanic culture(s) and draw appropriate educational implications from them. In contrast, teachers lacking cultural sensitivity and appreciation will have difficulty recognizing their Hispanic students' needs and consequently have a difficult time helping their students meet those needs.

Diversity

Cultural Diversity

The task of informing oneself about cultures other than one's own is complicated by the fact that there is great variability within all cultural and economic groups. This is because group membership is not about absolutes, but rather membership reflects multiple dimensions of peoples' lives that are determined in part by culture, socioeconomic class, gender, sexual orientation, and language.

This means that there are Hispanic children who come from economically privileged homes, middle-class homes, working class homes, and homes in poverty. Equally important, Hispanic children on any given economic level may have more in common with other children of the same economic level than they do with children of the same cultural background but different economic class.

Diversity: From Traditional to Assimilated

Another complicating feature in developing cultural sensitivity is *assimilation*—the degree to which a person has taken on the dominate culture within which they live. For many Hispanics, this is white mainstream society.

Assimilation is important because a child's degree of assimilation is central to understanding the child and her needs because there is tremendous variability in assimilation among children in any given community. People range from highly traditional to totally assimilated.

The culturally sensitive teacher, in other words, is aware of two things. First, cultural diversity is seen against the background of the teacher's own culture—and so being cognizant of one's own cultural values, traditions, and behaviors helps determine how culturally sensitive a person can be. And second, there is tremendous cultural variability among children in a community; this variability is due to a range of factors, including but not limited to age, race and ethnicity, economics, and assimilation. There is another important contributor to cultural sensitivity and it is to that issue we now turn.

Socioeconomic Factors

Poverty is an important contributor to diversity in public school classrooms. Variability in family financial resources contributes to diversity in two ways. First, family financial status is related to the presence (and absence) of educational opportunities available to children. Second, one-fifth of all children live in poverty with the figure being much greater for preschoolers and children of "minority" groups (e.g., Hispanics in some communities). And there are many more children in families living just above the poverty line ("the working poor") who must also be considered when exploring the impact of economics on the education of children (O'Hare, 1996).

As noted earlier, families in a given social class share much in common with the families from other cultures groups in the same social class. The parents of middle-class Hispanics generally relate well to the school, teacher, and other school personnel just like mainstream culture, middle-class parents. They will attend parent–teacher conferences, and serve on committees. Please note that this does not mean that these parents are totally assimilated into the mainstream culture. They may, however, well have the advantage of being bicultural.

Children of Migrant Families

Jose Luis Rios, a third-grader, describes being a child of migrant workers:

> When I work in the fields I don't get paid. I don't want to get paid because that's not good. They pay my family for what I pick.... But sometimes it is hard and I'm tired in school on Monday because I worked on the weekend. I also get a lot of bad headaches, so sometimes I have to leave school early or go rest in the nurse's office. When my father took me to the fields last year during the week, it was hard to work and go to school at the same time. (Atkin, 1993 pp. 14–15).

Children of migrant families are exposed to another factor that contributes to diversity—their life is transitory nature and their income doesn't cover the needs of the family. Not all migrant children have the luxury of regularly attending a given school, and this lack of educational continuity creates educational and social problems. While there are several excellent programs that help track the academic progress of migrant students and share these records with the students' next schools, many migrant students nevertheless fall through the cracks in the system. This is important because the migratory nature of the students' lives predisposes them to the alienation they may feel in the classroom. The short tenure in a given classroom and their poverty makes it harder for them to feel comfortable in their new classrooms and so may result in rejection by their classmates and the school. Ann Cranston-Gringras, director for The Center for the Study of Migrant Education at the University of South Florida reports,

> One of the things we've heard a lot from kids and one of the things we see, is that a lot of schools feel like migrants are not really their responsibility.... Migrant kids are going to move on, so nobody takes ownership. The kids don't feel a part of the school, and they become alienated. (quoted in Johanneson, 1999, p. 34)

Being good teachers of children from diverse backgrounds requires cultural sensitivity and an appreciation of how economics impacts people's lives. Cultural sensitivity and an understanding of economic impacts are especially important in the case of children from migrant families.

Factors That Influence Hispanic Students' Learning

Cultural Sensitivity and Classroom Expectations

Existing classroom programs are designed to meet the needs of children from mainstream, middle-class society. Indeed, appropriate classroom behaviors—whether those of the teachers or the students—are generally those agreed on by the dominant culture, and they are accepted largely because they carry the weight of tradition. This means that Hispanic and other children who aren't white and middle class may well be handicapped before they even step into a classroom.They won't know what's expected of them unless they are highly assimilated or bicultural. These students will be asked to play by rules they neither know nor understand as they try to address their academic and social needs in the school. This situation is simply not equitable.

Equity and Effective Teaching

Please note that *equity* is not synonymous with "equal." Equity means meeting the needs of each individual child (even though some children have greater needs than others) while equality means providing all children with the same opportunities and resources. The child whose environment lacks the resources and opportunities of their classmates may have greater needs and consequently require more time and resources than other children. Equity, in short, does not mean treating all children exactly the same but rather meeting their needs so that they have an equal opportunity for success (Fuller, 2000).

Stereotyping

Identifying cultural characteristics is an important activity if teachers are to be culturally sensitive. The risk here is that there is great diversity within the Hispanic cultures and so it is impossible to describe completely all the people in a single group—let alone describe all the people who belong to different Hispanic cultures (Mexican, Puerto Rican, Cuban, etc.). The risk matures into a problem when the cultural description goes from being a generalization to an *overgeneralization* commonly called a *stereotype*. Stereotypes and stereotyping are harmful because they ignore the variability that exists within a culture and in doing so limit what the observer sees and expects of a group. The danger in using stereotypes is that they limit educators' (and others') expectations of the children they encounter.

Stereotyping also causes problems for both teachers and their students because a single, narrow description is forced to apply in all circumstances. The result in these cases is that simple observations are offered for complex cultural phenomena. Further, behaviors not fitting the stereotype will appear arbitrary and uninterpretable and, when this happens, teachers will be at a disadvantage in planning appropriate educational strategies.

AUTHOR'S NOTE **Mary Lou Fuller**

Generalizations can be helpful but they are restrictive. When I visited rural areas of Thailand I was told that it was socially unacceptable to point the soles of my feet at people (in Buddhism, the head is holy and the feet least holy). Since I cross my legs when I sit, I had to be constantly vigilant. In rural Morocco I dressed as modestly as possible and went nowhere without a male escort. These generalizations didn't make me culturally literate but they helped me operate in other cultures.

Culture and Educational Implications

Being knowledgeable about, and appreciative of Hispanic cultures and issues bearing on children within Hispanic communities is an important first step in the journey to being a good teacher for Hispanic children. The second step is one of developing teaching strategies based on those issues that are appropriate to classrooms with Hispanic students. We begin by first identifying factors that must be considered in understanding Hispanic children and then identify teaching strategies that are sensitive to the needs of these students.

Cultural Traits

Family, community, and ethnic group are all central to the lives of most Hispanic students. The family is commonly the most valued of these institutions, and inspires great loyalty. Consistent with this fact, Hispanic parents tend to be affectionate and nurturing, and in addition, the extended family often plays a more active role in the lives of Hispanic children than in the Euro-American families.

Age and gender are usually important factors in determining each individual's status in the community, and sex roles are often more clearly defined than in the larger society. There is an emphasis on feminity for girls, and in highly traditional homes submissiveness. Boys are given more autonomy and expected to be loyal to, and responsible for, their family and community (Carrasquillo, 1991; Lockwood & Secada, 1999; Sosa, 1991).

Hispanic children often develop a strong sense of community. They are generally taught to be cooperative and to be good members of their cultural groups (Connoly & Tucker, 1982; Reyes, Scribner, & Scribner, 1999). This means that as students, Hispanic children tend to be more warm, concerned about others, and physically affectionate than children from the mainstream society (e.g., touching is an important part of interpersonal communication in the culture). This means that the required distance between people (also called *personal space*) is often much less than it is in the mainstream society with handshakes frequent among acquaintances and hugs common among family members and close friends.

AUTHOR'S NOTES **Mary Lou Fuller**

As part of an undergraduate multicultural class, my students were corresponding with a like class at another university. While my students were all of northern

European backgrounds, the other class was primarily Hispanic. Some interesting stories emerged as they talked over their cultural characteristics with one another. One of my students said that her father went to a reunion where he saw two brothers he hadn't seen for many years and the men shook hands when they met. For her culture that was appropriate. The Hispanic students were surprised and shared that in a like situation their fathers and uncles would have hugged one another and been emotional. Both groups began to identify characteristics of their own culture and learned to appreciate that cultural behavior that differed from what they were used to were not anomalies but differences in adapting to their respective environments.

Professional Moment

Before proceeding, consider each of the cultural characteristics mentioned above the make a list of possible classroom implications. How do they compare to the suggestions below?

Classroom Implications

What Teachers Can Expect

Because Hispanic children respect adults and have a respect for age, the teacher is expected to play a positive role and be an authority figure. And because of their status in the community, teachers receive respect and appreciation.

Classrooms. Although competition and individualism are traditions in most U.S. schools, many Hispanic children will feel more comfortable in a cooperative environment (Carrasquillo, 1991; Reyes, Scribner, & Scribner, 1999). Thus wise teachers will plan accordingly for Hispanic children because tensions caused by differences between their cultural preferences and the traditions of the school can only result in frustration for both the students and the teachers.

The question, then, is how do you go about creating a cooperative attitude in the classroom? This can be accomplished by pointing out that good behavior reflects on the whole class and, whenever possible, by implementing group problem solving. William Glasser's (1987) earlier works and his control theory are particularly appropriate for most Hispanic classrooms for it integrates nicely with cooperative learning (Jones & Jones, 1997). The teacher's role in such a classroom is to be active and nurturing;

in fact, it is not unlike a parent's role, and this encourages and supports a "sense of group" within the class (Reyes, Scribner, & Scribner, 1999).

Teachers will want to be physically affectionate with their students in age and gender appropriate ways. This includes a hand on the arm while talking, a pat on the shoulder while passing, a hug to comfort or affirm, or a smile across the classroom. All in all, Hispanic children will benefit from a warm, friendly classroom.

Classroom Management. It is often demeaning for a Hispanic child to be publicly disciplined—as is true for most children—because the power of the group is strong. Further, the purpose of discipline for children should be to change a behavior (as opposed to punishing a child) and should be done away from the group whenever possible.

On Noting Cultural Differences

Sometimes the most important thing for a teacher to do is recognize and understand the educational significance of cultural characteristics. This is important because, unfortunately, some teachers feel that recognition of diversity is somehow undemocratic and evidence of bias. These teachers assert that all children are alike: "I don't see color; I see children and I treat them all the same" is what they will say.

AUTHOR'S NOTE **Mary Lou Fuller**

I saw an example of this when I visited a classroom in the Southwest where all of the students save two were Mexican American. When I mentioned this to the teacher, she responded, with great pride, "I hadn't noticed."

This truism reflected her attitude toward her students. Her classroom strategies and environment did not acknowledge the cultures in which her students lived. By not acknowledging that there were Hispanic students in her classroom, the intellectual and physical environments told her students—both Mexican-American and Euro-American—that the Mexican culture was simply not important to acknowledge.

Gloria Ladson-Billings asserts that

> these attempts at color-blindness mask "dysconscious racism," an uncritical habit of mind that justifies inequity and exploitation by accepting the existing order (1994, p. 25).

She goes on to say,

> This is not to suggest that these teachers are racist in the conventional sense. They do not consciously deprive or punish "African-American" children [or Hispanic children] on the basis of their race, but at the same time they are not conscious of the ways in which some children are privileged and others are disadvantaged in the classroom. Their "dysconsciousness" comes to play when they fail to challenge the status quo, when they accept the given as inevitable (Ladson-Billings, 1994, p. 25)

More is involved here than simply denying the legitimacy of children's cultures. As noted earlier, when significant differences exist between the students' and the teacher's culture, they can easily misread students' values, perspectives, understandings, intent, language use, and interactional patterns—with teachers often interpreting what they see as deficient. Having misinterpreted students in this way, teachers also risk choosing instructional and/or disciplinary strategies and tactics that are at odds with the communities from which the children come (Delpit, 1995).

Educational Strategies

Creating a Positive Learning Environment

Cultural knowledge and sensitivity provide teachers with the knowledge and insights they need to address the requirements of children from diverse backgrounds. This knowledge needs to be applied before children can benefit from it, and it is to that application that we now turn. These applications seek to arrange the physical and emotional environments so they support learning, and so we will consider them. Since the educator's attitude also impacts on how children do, we'll address it as well (Fuller 2000).

Physical Environment

Two aspects of the physical environment are of particular importance in ensuring that Hispanic children are supported in their learning activities: Their 'worlds' must be seen as valuable (and valued), and they must have the opportunity to be active.

Reflecting the Students' World. Classrooms in which Hispanic students are comfortable learning allows these children to see themselves both culturally and geographically. The classroom, in other words, is a place where they can see themselves, their communities, and since Hispanic children are themselves highly varied, the ways in which their communities relate to other Hispanic groups. This reflection of Hispanic heritage should appear in the textbooks and the trade books found in their classroom since this kind of information allows the children to see themselves as well as others (Fuller, 2000).

An important way of making children comfortable in their classroom is to display their work and have them help decorate the room. Certainly, some of what they display will describe their homes and their communities, but other things can be represented as well. These might also include things the children do that they share with all other kids—regardless of ethnic or economic background—such as sports or music. A problem appears when non-Hispanic kinds of things appear to the exclusion of everything else.

AUTHOR'S NOTE **Mary Lou Fuller**

I once visited a fifth grade classroom on the New Mexico–Mexican border. The room displayed pictures of colonial Jamestown and because it was springtime the bulletin board was surrounded by paper tulips. In fact, when I looked at the calendar, I realized that it was May 5 (*Cinco de Mayo*) and that there was nothing in the classroom commemorating this holiday. Also, as much as I like tulips, I found those on the bulleting board paled in contrast to the Mexican golden poppies and other beautiful desert flowers that surrounded the school but didn't make it into the classroom.

For all children—but especially for those Hispanic kids who learn best when they can be physically active—the absence of space in which to move carries major classroom management implications. This includes the fact that not providing these kinds of opportunities predisposes some children toward a variety of disruptive behaviors.

Skillful teachers arrange their classrooms so that movement is encouraged. This means that (1) the class library, science area, computers center, and so on, are placed in various parts of the room with clear and visible paths leading to them, and (2) children are taught how to use the centers without disturbing others. It is also true that these same teachers plan activities requiring their students to move about between sedentary lessons. They also know that since some children need more physical movement than others, these kids should be not only allowed to move about, but they should be encouraged to do so.

Emotional Environment

As important as physical aspects of the classroom may be, the affective environment is likely even more important. We've already considered how to make the classroom a reflection of the Hispanic students' lives and communities, and this is necessary but not sufficient for teachers who wish Hispanic children to feel comfortable their classrooms. While children must be able to see themselves in a classroom environment, they must also be able to feel emotionally comfortable in that classroom. One way in which to do this is to ensure they feel a sense of community in the classroom.

Sense of Community. This will happen if children share a sense of unity which fosters respect for self and others. Many Hispanics value being a part of a community and when this sense of community is present in the classroom Hispanic children feel familiar and comfortable with the classroom structure—an environment within which they can learn to work, play, and solve problems. Referring to the class as "our" class helps build a sense of community, and the relationships that develop between the children and adults should be reminiscent of those of a family. For example, the children will be encouraged to take pride in the group's accomplishments as well as those of individuals.

Teacher Expectations

Research has shown that teachers' expectations for students tend to be self-fulfilling prophesies. Jere Brophy (1997) therefore advises teachers to routinely project attitudes, beliefs, expectations, and attributions that imply that your students share your own enthusiasm for learning and that you treat your students as if they already are eager learners.

There is a large body of literature supporting the positive effects of teacher expectations on the students of diversity's learning and sense of self (Brophy, 1997; Hamachek, 1995; Wise, 1996). And although Cleary and Peacock (1998) speak specifically to the needs of Native American children, their observations are also timely for Hispanic children. They stress that an important part of having high expectations of children involves knowing where they are academically and having a clear goal of where you want them to be—and also setting clear goals that haven't been watered down. Obviously, having high expectations does not magically increase students' innate abilities and learning rates but it does help children come closer to meeting their own potentials.

"All in all, teachers see what they expect to see, and students see what the teacher sees" (Hamachek, 1995, p. 56). In other words, teacher expectations becomes students' self-perceptions. And while this is true generally, it is particularly important for teachers working with children of color and children from low income families. The danger for teachers in these situations is that lack of cultural sensitivity is often associated with holding lower expectations for these students—and the students respond by acting in ways that reflect those reduced expectations.

Eugene E. Garcia in his book *Hispanic Education in the United States: Raices y Alas* provides us with a beautiful description of the effects of teacher expectation.

> For me it was a critical set of teachers—teachers who did recognize my talents and challenged me to a higher standard. Most teachers did not expect much of me. I was quiet, spoke enough English to get by, but was not articulate in English, and it was evident that I was poor and came from a background of "educational disadvantage." It seems that this should have signaled to educators that I might need "more" help than the average student might. Instead it seemed to signal to them they should expect less than what they expected of their "gifted" students. And I obliged them...I learned not to work very hard in my studies, to get by, and to do as many of my Hispanic peers did, namely, to look elsewhere for opportunities—in sports, in gangs, or in work, but not in academic aspects of schooling. It was several Spanish teachers and several athletic coaches who were the exception. They were my lucky charms. (Garcia, 2001, p. 126)

Garcia goes on to discuss the academic and social fate of his Hispanic peers, particularly males, referring to those Hispanic students for whom low expectation due to their cultural and economic background, was the rule:

> This was not the experience of many of my Spanish-speaking or bilingual peers, children of the same neighborhood.... For them school was a "real drag." For them, defending our turf and assuring respect for our "barrio" and making money usually through illegal means (that was all that was available to us) led to the formation of and participation in gangs. (Garcia, 2001, p. 127)

In other words, they met the expectations of their educational experience.

Guidelines for Teaching Hispanic Children

Alicia Sosa in her book *Thorough and Fair: Creating Routes to Success for Mexican-American Students* (1993, pp. 24–25), proposes a variety of factors which contribute to a successful school experience for Hispanic students. We would like to encourage our readers to make a copy of the list below and use it as a guide for their instruction of Hispanic students. Use it in the planning for the school year and then check it frequently to see which areas need more time and attention and then plan accordingly. If you follow Sosa's guidelines you will have done much to create a culturally sensitive classroom for Hispanic children.

Curriculum

- Textbook materials and lessons validate students' culture and history.
- Lessons are organized using thematic units.
- Curriculum promotes higher-order thinking skills.
- Language learning is promoted.
- Maximum use is made of group work.

Instruction

- Students' language and culture are valued.
- Teachers impart high expectations and provide strong support.
- Teachers use students' background and strengths in planning and implementing and teaching episodes, making use of learning styles and collaborative work.
- Through interactive teaching, teachers provide opportunities for students to talk and write as a way to learn.
- Teachers develop students' higher order thinking skills.
- A highly informal, family-like atmosphere exists, in which students help each other learn.

Assessment

- Teacher and the principal monitor student progress.
- Assessment is conducted in the native language when appropriate.
- Testing is used for diagnostic purposes, to target help for students, not to justify inaction.
- On average, students are achieving at or very close to grade level (in either language).

Summary

Eugene Garcia (2001) reports on a synthesis of research covering appropriate strategies in teaching Hispanic children. Not surprisingly, teachers are the most important factor in the success of Hispanic children's educational experiences. The following is part of this synthesis of research and also covers the major points made in this chapter and Chapter 7: (1) teach content so that it interests and challenges Hispanic students; (2) communicate high expectations, respects, and interest in each of their students; (3) understand the roles of languages, race, culture, and gender in schooling; (4) engage parents and community in the education of their children; and (5) be knowledgeable about developing strategies to educate Hispanic students and to communicate with their parents.

While there are no formulas for teaching Hispanic students (or any other group) there are things that can help you develop a culturally sensitive and an academically productive classroom. You must know the culture of your students (and the language, if possible) and your classroom must reflect this knowledge. You also must understand the diversity of your classroom (socioeconomics status, degree of assimilation, individual needs, community, etc.), and be able to understand how this diversity effects Hispanic students and teach accordingly. Preparing to teach children of a culture that differs from your own is time consuming and hard work but the rewards are far greater than the effort.

REFERENCES

Atkins, S. B. (1993). *Voices from the fields.* New York: Scholastic Inc.

Brophy, J. E. (1997). *Motivating students to learn.* New York: McGraw-Hill

Carrasquillo, A. L. (1991). *Hispanic children and youth in the United States.* New York: Garland Publishing, Inc.

Cleary, L. M., and Peacock, T. D. (1998). *Collected wisdom.* Boston: Allyn & Bacon.

Connoly, L. H., & Tucker, S. M. (1982). *Motivating the Mexican American student.* Las Cruces, NM: ERIC Clearinghouse on Rural Education and Small Schools. (ERIC Document Reproduction Service No. ED 287 0657).

Delpit, L. (1995). *Other people's children.* New York: The New Press.

Dodd, J. M., Nelson, J. R., & Peralez, E. (1989). Understanding the Hispanic student. *Rural Educator, 10*(2), 8–13.

Fuller, M. L. (2000). Culturally sensitive classroom management. In C. Grant and M. L. Gomez (eds.), *Campus and classrooms: Making schools multicultural,* 2nd ed. Columbus: Merrill Publishing Company,

Garcia, E. E. (2001) *Hispanic education in the United States: Raices y Alas.* Lanham, MD: Rowman & Littlefield Publishing.

Glasser, W. (1987). *Control theory in the classroom.* New York: HarperCollins.

Glazer, N., and Moynihan, D. P. (1991). *Beyond the melting pot,* 2nd ed. Boston: MIT Press.

Hamachek, D. E. (1995). *Psychology of teaching, learning, and growth.* Boston: Allyn & Bacon.

Johanneson, A.S. (1999). Follow the stream. *Teaching Tolerance (15),* 34.

Jones, V. F., & Jones, L. S. (1997). *Comprehensive classrooms: Creating communities of support and solving problems.* Boston: Allyn & Bacon.

Ladson-Billings, G. (1994) *The dreamkeepers: Successful teachers of African American children.* San Francisco: Jossey Bass.

Lockwood, A. T., & Secada, W. G. (1999). Transforming education for Hispanic youth: Exemplary practices, programs, and schools. NCBE (National Clearinghouse for Bilingual Education) *Resource Collection Series 12*(1).

O'Hare, W. (1996). The new look at poverty in America. *Population Bulletin,* 51, 2.

Reyes, P., Scribner, J. D., Scribner, A. P. (1999). *Lessons from high-performing Hispanic schools: Creating learning communities.* New York: Teacher's College Press.

Sosa, A. (1993). *Thorough and fair: Creating routes to success for Mexican-American students.* Charleston, WV: ERIC Clearinghouse/Rural Education and Small Schools.

Valdez, G. (1996). *Con respeto: Bridging the distance between culturally diverse families and schools: An ethnographic portrait.* New York: Teacher's College Press.

Wise, A. E. (1996). Shattering the status quo: The National Commission report on teacher preparation, *NCATE: Quality Teaching, 6,* 1.

CHAPTER

7 Hispanic Families

It's been my dream for many years to make a film about a Latino family. We aren't just individuals; we are each a product of our families. Familia is the very center of Latino culture. I don't feel the media has really seen that. It is the strongest thing about us and the most universal.

—Gregory Nava, filmmaker

This chapter covers the following topics:

- The nature and responsibilities of families
- The diversity of hispanic families
- Families and the school community
- Cultural characteristics of the traditional family
- Parental involvement
- Families, their children, and the school

Families are the most important institution in the Hispanic cultures, and without understanding the family you cannot understand your Hispanic students. Understanding students' families sounds like a simple task as we have all had experiences with families—primarily with our nuclear families and to a lesser extent with our extended families, and of course our friends and neighbors families. Unfortunately, understanding our students' families is not that simple.

Each family is unique even though all families have much in common. Families all address the same goals though how these goals are met may differ dramatically. The structure of the family for example, varies greatly, your students may live in families that are intact,[1] while others are in

[1]*Intact* is not a value judgment but rather a sociological term used to describe families with the original parents and their birth or adopted children.

blended families, still others are in single parent families, or they may also live in families headed by grandparents, the parents may be gay or lesbian parents, or temporary families as experienced by children in foster families in addition to numerous other structures. And to make matters even more complex, there is great diversity within each of these family structures. As an example, the national step-parenting organization has identified 37 different kinds of step families.

The Responsibilities of Families: To Prepare and Protect

Families are like all of societies important institutions in that they are forever changing. Families are like the cultures within which they function—they are never static. In fact the family is in some respects a microcosm of society, reflecting within its many facets the social, economic, and legal aspects of society, at large. But most important the family is the primary agent of enculturation (Carrasquillo, 1991).

To Prepare: Enculturation

What is enculturation? Consider for a moment: how do you know how to act in a place of worship, at a museum, at a party with strangers, or at a family reunion with people you have known for years? Though one gets no formal instructions on behavior in these settings, most people know exactly what is expected of them and act accordingly. Children learn these skills both through receiving parental guidance and by observing members of their family and others as they interact in various societal settings. Anthropologists refer to learning in this way as *enculturation*—the process by which a family and/or society let children know what's expected of them and prepares children to behave appropriately and appreciate their cultural values and traditions. The result of enculturation ensures that people in a given society understand and can interact with others from the same society. Hispanic children are like children everywhere: they get the essence of their culture from those closest to them—they learn what it means to be Hispanic.

To Protect

Protecting children has always been a primary responsibility of the family. Parents a thousand generations ago did what parents basically do today—what's changed is the threats their children face—no concern now about wild animals, but children learn to stay off busy streets. The natures of the dangers may look very different from those of early families but the responsibilities remain the same. Parents create the safest environment within their power.

Diversity among and between Families

Though most people think of children when they think of families, only 37 percent of all families in the United States have minor children in their homes, and this number is expected to decrease to 34 percent in the next five years. Moreover, and noted earlier, there is considerable diversity within that 37 percent (Ahlburg & DeVita, 1995).

Since the Mexican population is a younger population than the white non-Hispanic population this group includes many younger families. As a result, they have more families with children than the older, white non-Hispanic population. (The census bureau defines families with children as those families who have children 18 years of age or younger and live with their parents.) Mexican families in the United States are also larger with 33.2 percent having five or more family members while the white non-Hispanic family has 11.8 percent (Therrien & Rameriz, 2000).

The role of the Hispanic family is very important in ensuring the success of their children. This is made more difficult by the fact that Hispanic children and youth face challenges related to family education, income and occupation, housing, family arrangements, and family social and economic dependence (Carrasquillo, 1991).

In 1999, for example, 22.8 percent of Hispanics were living in poverty as opposed to 7 percent of the white non-Hispanic population. And this percent is larger when you look at the number of children living in poverty: An appalling 30.3 percent of Hispanic children live in poverty as opposed to 7 percent of the white non-Hispanic children. (These figures vary when breaking down Hispanics into individual cultures with higher percentages of Mexicans and Puerto Ricans living in poverty than Cubans (Therrien & Rameriz, 2000). Poverty is an important consideration. Besides the lack of resources to receive proper health care, nutrition, day care, and so on, children who live below the poverty line are also likely to live in substandard housing, in neighborhoods with a disproportionate amount of violence, and attend public schools that lack the resources of middle-class suburban schools.

Families and the School Community

The home environment is often cited as the reason for lack of academic achievement among low-income students—with parents being criticized for being insufficiently involved. This perspective fails to understand both these families and the effects of insufficient resources. Finding money for food, clothing, housing, and health care, command larger amounts of the time and energy of low-income parents than the parents in middle-class communities. The result is that these parents are often too invested in survival issues to attend to the educational needs of their children (Ascher, 1988).

People who are not middle-class also have expectations for the schools and how they'll interact with the schools that are different from the expectations the schools have for them. When these expectations do not agree, parents are often precluded from involvement with the school (Ornstein & Levine, 1989).

AUTHOR'S NOTE **Mary Lou Fuller**

My preservice teachers were white, middle class, and very few had a significant relationship with another culture. Even though they were academically prepared for other cultures, they felt uncomfortable about working with parents of cultures that differed from theirs. However, after working with Hispanic parents their responses were almost predictable.

First, they were impressed by the way their Hispanic children looked. They would tell me how cute they were and comment "The parents send the children to school sparkling clean and neat [cleanliness is an important value in the preservice teachers' cultures] and the kids are dressed so nicely."

Then they would tell me how much the parents appreciated them individually and respected teachers generally. A story that I often heard had to do with school parties. The mothers, and sometimes aunts, grandmothers, and younger children would come to the parties and bring great quantities of food.

Unlike middle-class peers, children living in poverty often experience discontinuity between what school expects of them and what they expect of the schools. Studies focusing on the relationship between socioeconomic status and academic success, for example, note that conventional standards for success in school are based on middle-class expectations. This means that students who lack middle-class experiences and opportunities available to children from middle-class families—through no fault of their own—won't benefit as much from school (Fuller & Olsen, 1998). This includes social and language behaviors and behaviors middle-class students' master prior to entering school. The consequences are that children of poverty enter schools that were designed for someone else and so they don't know what's expected of them. Planning for more successful school experiences for Hispanic children is very difficult without an understanding of this phenomenon.

Traditional and Assimilated

Perhaps the two most important factors influencing the Hispanic family and how they will function are the resources available to the family (as we've already seen) and where they are on the cultural continuum from traditional too assimilated. The continuum, as far as schools are concerned, considers how well the family functions in the mainstream society and so it is impossible to understand Hispanic families without examining the degree of their cultural involvement.

Because of the great diversity within and among cultures, it is impossible to describe any group absolutely, and so the following observations must be understood as generalizations. The following are applicable to Mexican families though they also apply to other Hispanic groups.

- The closer a Mexican-American family lives to the Mexican border the more apt they are to be culturally traditional.
- Another factor is the size of the Mexican-American community—the larger the community of Mexican Americans the more traditional they tend to be.
- And last, the length of time they have lived in the United States—the more recent a Mexican's entry into the United States the more culturally traditional they will tend to be. The opposite would suggest that if Hispanics live a great distance from their native country, in a community where there are few other Hispanics, and have lived in the United States for a considerable period, they will tend to be more assimilated than traditional.

Migrant Workers

An area of familial diversity that is part of the Hispanic population consists of Migrant families. This group face unique challenges educating their children, challenges that are sometimes misunderstood by educators. Although there are some excellent programs for migrant children, many migrant children find that these programs are not available to them. Absent these kinds of programs, migrant children suffer from lack of continuity in their education. The migration of field workers isolate the family, thus, strengthening family ties. One way migrant families deal with financial problems is to ask their children to stay home from school and care for the younger children while their parents are in the field working (UC Davis Health System, 2000).

Migrant workers also face other issues. Because both parents work in these families, household tasks must be distributed, and this leads to more flexible male and female roles. Interestingly there is an uncommon generosity found in this poor population. This means it is common for a migrant family to share their limited resources (food, housing, etc.) with other migrant families (Valdes, 1996).

Migrant families suffer many hardships in order to feed, dress, and educate their children. Ten-year-old Manuel Araizia shares some of his family's experiences in coming to this country.

> When I was five my whole family came here, over the hills and across the border. We paid someone to take us. A coyote. I felt bad when we went over the hills, scared too. We walked and walked all night, and then we got into a car that the coyote had hidden. We got in the back of the car...and he took us to Tijuana.... [And there] my father picked us up in another car.
>
> Our house here is one room with a kitchen. We used to have a bathroom in our house in Mexico but here the bathroom is outside and we share it with the other families (11 or 12). (Atkins, 1993, p. 29–30)

The reality is that families like Manuel's arrive in this country and establish themselves. It is not an easy existence for them, but this does serve to bring families closer—to build bonds among its members (Valdes, 1996). Victor Machuca, age 15, describes what this means to him.

> When my parents get older, if they can't work, I'll help them. They always help me and have given me food since I was little, so I would like to do the same for them. Sometimes now I would like to be able to give them money. If I were making, let's say, fifty dollars a week I would give all the money to them and they would give me back what I need. I think my friends feel like I do about their families. Their parents are important to them, and they listen to their advice.... When I get older, I want to live close to my family, all of them. There isn't anything more important than family. (Atkins, 1993, p. 53)

Guadalupe Valdes (1996), did an ethnographic study of ten migrant families. One of the conclusions she reached was that although teachers tried their best to help migrant children they appeared to have failed. This is likely because the skills these children brought from home seem inappropriate in the school setting and the children's parents felt helpless and confused.

This is an example of the school and the migrant parents making erroneous assumptions about one another. The schools expected migrant children to exhibit middle-class characteristics although the parents had limited knowledge of what was expected of them and were worried about communicating with teachers. The parents were concerned that their English was inadequate and if they wrote notes this would reflect poorly on them.

The teachers felt that children should come to school with certain skills and the parents assumed that teaching children those skills was the teacher's responsibility. In addition, the physical realities of the parents' lives were out of the realm of the teachers' experiences. At the same time, and because the parents had little formal schooling, they didn't know what to expect of the school. A common complaint of teachers of migrant children (and indeed teachers of children from other low income Hispanic families), is that often the parents don't attend parent teacher conferences. This is another example of problems arising when the parents and the teachers don't share an agreed on set of expectations for one another (Valdes, 1996).

But who takes the leads in establishing mutual understanding? We believe that it is our responsibility as educators to understand the students and their families, and this in turn spells out some additional tasks for us. We must gather general knowledge about the lives and educational expectations of migrant families and then use what we learn to understand individual students and their families.

Cultural Characteristics Often Exhibited by More Traditional Families

In the year 2000, one out of four Hispanics were naturalized citizens, in other words, 1/4 were foreign born (Therrien & Ramirez, 2001). This is particularly significant as naturalized citizens are normally closer to their cultural roots (e.g., they haven't been in this country as long) than native-born Hispanic citizens. Understanding another culture is a long and complicated process especially for migrants who are not well educated. Culture must also include history, art, literature, language, locale, behavior, and so on. Culture is learned and includes the way we act, think, and feel.

The danger in brief definitions of culture is that these generalizations may become stereotypes. However, it would be unthinkable to talk about Hispanic families, especially the more traditional families, without addressing the warmth, sharing, and dedication they have toward one another. With this caveat consider the following cultural characteristics.

The California Identity Project found that Hispanics in the United States continued to practice their cultural traditions into the third generation. More than 96 percent base their identity on their family and 84 percent felt the culture was an important part of their identity. Also included were identification with the Catholic church (76 percent) and being Spanish speakers (67 percent). "In contrast to the European immigrants, Hispanics continue to base their identity on the family, culture, religion and language" (Olmos, Yberra, & Monterrey, 1999, p. 40).

Children. Children are raised in a protective environment and are expected to be obedient and respectful. Hard work and achievement is encouraged with the expectation that the next generation will "do better" than the current one. Children are especially traumatized by separation from family members. (Olmos, Yberra, & Monterrey, 1999; UC Davis Health System, 2000).

Gender Roles. The discussion of gender roles for Hispanics is too often one of stereotypes. The passive, meek woman and the tough, insensitive, macho man. They fit in the same genre as the Mexican man wearing a large sombrero, leaning against a saguaro cactus. In their wonderful book, *Americanos: Latino Life in the United States,* Olmos, Yberra, and Monterrey stressed the importance of the family and discussed gender behaviors.

> A discussion of the Latino family is incomplete without recognition of the central role Latina women have played in both the family and community. Despite the stereotypical portrayal of Latinas as passive women, they have always been a source of strength for family members. They maintain and nurture strong familial ties and loyalty. Historically, many Latinas also have been involved outside the family sphere in educational community, and labor activities.... Latinas are a diverse and dynamic group of women.... As grandmothers, mothers, and daughters, single, divorced, or married, they are the cornerstones of family life.

Olmos, Yberra, and Monterrey go on to say:

> We also must consider the role of the male in the Latino family. As there are several definitions of the Latino family there are several definitions of machismo. But that of the macho as womanizer and abuser too often has been in the forefront...many Latinos men exemplify the positive definition of a macho as one who works hard, values his family, and has valor, dignity and honor (1999, p. 84).

Family Orientation. A strong sense of loyalty, reciprocity, and solidarity exists among family members. The behavior of the individual family members is mediated by concerns for the reputation of the entire family. (Olmos, Yberra, Monterrey, 1999; UC Davis Health System, 2000).

Respect for Elders. The Mexican American culture maintains reverence for elders; elders are treated respectfully and often in a formal manner. Elders may be actively involved in the care and education of children (Reyes, Scribner, & Scribner, 1999; UC Davis Health System, 2000).

Extended Family. The importance of family structure and support for extended families remains strong. Hispanic children are normally nurtured with great care by a large number of relatives at home (Inger 1992; Olmos, Yberra, & Monterrey, 1999).

Professional Moment

Gregory Nava (quoted at the beginning of the chapter) wished he could make a movie about a Hispanic family that would demonstrate the importance of the role that the family has. He did make the movie and *Mi Familia* was the recipient of many awards and excellent reviews. See this movie and document the cultural characteristics listed above.

Parental Involvement

There is considerable evidence that parent involvement leads to improved student achievement, better school attendance, and reduced dropout rates. What's more, these improvements occur regardless of the economic, racial, or cultural background of the child (Flaxman & Inger, 1991).

What is parent involvement? This is an important question because Hispanic parents may perceive parent involvement differently than the schools their children attend. Educators in *Lessons from High-Performing Hispanic Schools* considered parent involvement an important way to serve the needs of both the school (volunteering, fund raising, etc.) and the children. While the Hispanic parents valued these activities, their primary concerns were to assist their children academically and socially, and to strengthen their relationship with the school. A secondary goal for the parents was to be available as volunteers and fund raisers (Reyes, Scribner, & Scribner, 1999). This has the potential for creating some serious misunderstanding and conflict between the two group. Consequently, the school must solicit the parents' perceptions of parental involvement and then share their own.

Parent involvement in primarily Hispanic schools must be negotiated between the home and the school. However, if the goals include the home and school collaborating for the good of the children, the basis for a good parent involvement program exists.

Problems

Many school administrators and teachers misread Hispanic reserve, the non-confrontational manners, and (as noted earlier) the noninvolvement of parents at school to mean that they are uncaring about their children's education—and this misperception has led to a cycle of mutual mistrust and suspicion between poor Hispanic parents and school personnel (Ovum & Navarette, 1990).

Families, Their Children, and School

Many educators are uncomfortable and uniformed about working with the parents of diverse student groups. On one hand, parental involvement is an important part of a successful classroom and is an excellent opportunity to learn about our students. On the other hand, we are afraid our lack of cultural knowledge might result in some great faux pas that will offend the parents and embarrass us. The best approach to this problem is to learn as much as possible about the children's families and cultures before meeting with their parents. General information can be collected through reading, and more specific information can be provided by administrators and other teachers at the school.

It is important to collect this information as it helps in approaching and understanding our students' families. Remember that teachers and parents already have a common bond: they both care about "their" child. It is for this reason that they should work as a team to provide the best education possible for the children. There are some things teachers can do to create a productive educational team: they should remember that these parents are sending them the best they have. They should convey to parents a genuine appreciation of their children. Educators need to create an environment where parents and teachers can work at understanding the parents' situations including family structure, socioeconomic level, work demands, culture, and so on.

Why should you as an educator be concerned about the family and how the people within it function? Henderson's research (1987) suggests three reasons. First, since your efforts at school relate to the efforts of the adults in your student's home lives, you need to know about your students' families to be maximally effective. Second, by understanding what the caregivers at home do, you can ensure they work with you at helping their children move comfortably into the school society. And third, you will simply become a better teacher.

Strategies That Work

The hardest part of building a partnership with low-income Hispanic parents is getting parents to the first meeting. Impersonal efforts—letters, flyers, announcements at church services or on local radio or TV—are largely ineffective, even when written in Spanish. The only successful approach is personal: face-to-face conversation with parents in their primary language and in their homes.

Home visits not only personalize the invitations but help you to better understand and deal with parents' concerns, including finding out who needs transportation, a baby sitter, an interpreter, and so on. Also home visits help build trust between the school and the home. Since many low income Hispanics feel uncomfortable in school, successful projects hold the first meetings outside the school, preferably at sites familiar to the parents. Successful first meetings are primarily social events; unsuccessful ones tend to be formal events at the school, with information aimed "at the parents" (Inger, 1992).

Culture and Community

Most of us have, at one time or another, found ourselves in situations in which we felt intimidated, uncomfortable, where we felt we just didn't belong. We didn't know what was expected of us, what the "unwritten rules" were, and making the situation even more uncomfortable—it was not predictable. This is how many Hispanic parents feel when they must meet with their child's teacher.

By building on the cultural values of our Hispanic student's families and being familiar with their home community we will have a good start at building a good working relationship with them.

Culture.

- Understanding cultural values
- Building on the strength of the extended family
- Making personal contact with parents
    - Creating opportunities for positive interaction
    - Engaging in small talk
    - Calling parents
    - Home visits

(Reyes, Scribner, & Scribner, 1999)

Community. It is also important to know your student's home community. Walk around the community and note the environment from which your students come, and if it is a rural area, ride the school bus—if your students take several different bus routes, ride each of the buses. Attend community functions. If there is a Cinco de Mayo celebration, a church bazaar, or an art fair, be there. It will give you a sense of the community as well as an opportunity to see your students in their home environment.

Participate in community functions. Know the issues facing your students' community and participate when appropriate. For example, you might participate in a "clean up campaign" or volunteer to help build a home in the Hispanic community through Habitat for Humanity.

Also, accept invitations to family events. You may be invited to a child's first communion, a quinceañera (celebration of a young girl's acceptance into the adult world, usually involving a mass and a party), and other family events. You will be well received and the family will be most appreciative that you joined them in their celebration and you'll find this an enjoyable learning experience.

Make homes visitations. Since the parent may not be comfortable in the teacher's school environment, visit them in an environment in which they are comfortable.

AUTHOR'S NOTE **Mary Lou Fuller**

In visiting my Hispanic students' homes I found that bringing cookies for the children was a good icebreaker. Hispanic parents, as most parents, appreciate acts of kindness to their children.

Also, most Hispanic families have photographs on the wall—often school pictures. Asking about the pictures is a good way of showing your interest in the family and gathering information. "Who is this handsome little boy? Is this Maria's brother?" or "What a wonderful old picture. Who are these people?"

Visit informally with the parents. When you meet your student's family in the mall, stop and visit with them. It should be just a casual conservation and not a mini-conference.

Don't make assumptions as to why a parent doesn't come to school. If you are working with low income Hispanics, you may have difficulty understanding their situation. Most teachers come from middle-class backgrounds with a limited understanding of the stresses and problems that are part of a limited household income. If you are dealing with middle-class Hispanics parents their school behaviors will generally reflect the behaviors of the other parents in the school.

In closing, we would like to share with you the attitude and practice of a school in Texas and suggest to you that if we all followed their dictate we would eliminate a number of problems that currently exist between the school and Hispanic parents.

> The familiar complaint that such an extended role for schools staff is not the schools' responsibility is not heard at Lennox Middle School. We do not lay the responsibility on the parents saying, "If he would just come to school" or "If she would only so this or that." Instead, responsibility for student achievement and engagement in school is shared. In this kind of support system, kids don't fall through the cracks. (Lockwood & Secada, 1999)

SUGGESTED ACTIVITIES

1. Study your own ethnicity and see how it has affected your perceptions and behaviors. Just because you do not celebrate national holidays of your country of origin or cook the foods of that area doesn't mean that you haven't been influenced by your ethnicity. A good place to start your quest for information is by interviewing older members of the family. Compare your cultural characteristics with those of Hispanic cultures. How are they the same and how so they differ?
2. Volunteer at a Hispanic Center to help in any way that you can, but preferably with family activities.
3. Make arrangements to tutor in a classroom that has a high percentage of Hispanic students and keep a journal of your experience.
4. Contact a Catholic church in an area with a large Hispanic population to determine if you might be able to work in a family-oriented project or organization.
5. Read the book *Americanos: Latino Life in the United States* by Olmos, Ybarra, and Monterrey. Through wonderful photographs of and narrative about Hispanic Americans it tells a story of the contemporary Hispanic in the United States. Select the ten pictures you feel are the most representative of the Hispanic culture and note why you selected them.
6. Take a class in Spanish to learn Spanish or improve your Spanish.

AUTHOR'S NOTE **Mary Lou Fuller**

I have had great success working with Catholic priests in congregations that were largely Hispanic. My preservice teachers tutored children, helped adults learn English, participated in planning and putting on Diá de los Muertos festivals, and so on. Some of the students formed ongoing relationships which continued after the class was completed.

REFERENCES

Ahlburg, D. A., & DeVita, C. (1995). New realities of the American family. *Population Bulletin, 47*, 2.

Ascher, C. (1988). Improving the school-home connection for poor and minority urban students. *The Urban Review, 20*(2), 109–123.

Atkins, S. B. (1993). *Voices from the fields*. New York: Scholastic Inc.

Carrasquillo, A. L. (1991). *Hispanic children and youth in the United States*. New York: Garland Publishing, Inc.

Flaxman, E., & Inger, M. (1991). Parents and schooling in the 1990s. *The Education Digest, 57*(9), 3–7.

Fuller, M. L., & Olsen, G. (1998). *Home school relations: Working successfully with families*. New York: Allyn & Bacon.

Gonzalez, R. (1996). *The fire in our souls*. New York: Plume.

Henderson, A. (1987). *The evidence continues to grow*. Columbia, MD: National Committee for Citizens in Education.

Inger, M. (1992). *Increasing the school involvement of Hispanic parents*. New York: ERIC No. ED 350-380.

Lockwood, A. T., & Secada, W. G. (1999). *Transforming education for Hispanic youth: Exemplary practices, programs, and schools*. University of Wisconsin–Madison: Resource Collection Series #12.

Olmos, E. J., Yberra, L., & Monterrey, M. (1999). *Americanos: Latino life in the United States*. New York: Little, Brown and Company.

Ornstein, A., & Levine, D. (1989). Social class, race, and school achievement: Problems, and prospects. *Journal of Teacher Education, 40*(5), 17–23.

Ovum, L., & Navarette, L. (1990). Project Excel: A national organization seeks to improve the American educational system for Hispanic children. *Electric Perspectives, 14*(1). ERIC No. ED 337-558.

Reyes, P., Scribner, J. D., & Scribner, A. P. (1990). *Lessons from high performing Hispanic schools: Creating learning communities*. New York: Teachers College Press.

Therrien, M., & Ramirez, R. R. (2000) *Current population in the United States. March 2000*. Washington, DC: U.S. Census Bureau.

UC Davis Health System (2000). *Mexican American family relationships*. www.udcmc.edu/edu/cultural/MexAm/family.htm.

Valdes, G. (1996). *Con respecto: Bridging the distance between culturally diverse families and schools*. New York: Teachers College Press.

CHAPTER

8 Resource Heaven

There are many excellent resources about Hispanic populations, their history, culture, practices, anything and everything you might want to know. The following resources are available to all teachers and we hope that readers will take advantage of all that is here. In our experience, one difficulty in teaching from a multicultural perspective for both new and experienced teachers is finding resources that are easily accessible and that we know are worthwhile. In this chapter we have collected a variety of resources that we have used or that have been recommended to us, so in a sense we have screened them for you. Some of the books, videos, and websites are for teachers and prospective teachers to use for their own growth and learning. Others are helpful to use directly with children or adolescents. Wherever we could, we have given information about where resources are available. Many of the books are also listed in reference lists with full bibliographic information at the end of previous chapters. The following resources are organized into categories to make it easier for teacher educators, preservice and inservice teachers to find them to use in their lessons.

- Annotated bibliography of books
- Suggested children's books
- Suggested adult fiction
- Movies about Hispanic populations
- Videos about Hispanic populations
- Websites
- Magazines and Other Periodicals

Annotated Bibliography of Books

Education

Hispanic Education in the United States (2001)
Eugene E. Garcia

Among the many recent books on educational reform, Eugene E. Garcia's *Hispanic Education in the United States* stands out as a landmark work.

Garcia vibrantly portrays "what works" in creating better educational opportunities and effective school reform. He also offers a telling reflection on the bicultural experience of minority groups in the United States. Culture is an asset in any individual's educational attainment. Garcia shows how and why our educational reforms must seek to build on rather than downplay the native culture and language of minority students. Poignant stories from the author's life—and from many other teachers and students—make this a vital book for the university classroom, and for any reader interested in the rapidly changing dynamics of America's schools.

Latinos and Education: A Critical Reader (1997)
Antonia Darder, Rodolfo D. Torres, and Henry Gutierrez (Eds.)

Despite generations of protest, activism, and reform efforts, Latinos continue to be among the nation's most educationally disadvantaged and economically disenfranchised groups. Challenging static notions of culture, identity, and language, *Latinos and Education* addresses this phenomenon within the context of a rapidly changing economy and society. This reader establishes a clear link between educational practice and the structural dimensions which shape institutional life, and calls for the development of a new language that moves beyond disciplinary and racialized categories of difference and structural inequality

Lessons from High-Performing Hispanic Schools: Creating Learning Communities (1999)
Pedro Reyes, Jay D. Scribner, and Alicia Paredes Scribner (Eds.)

This practical volume provides school administrators and teachers with the tools they need to transform ordinary schools into high performing schools. It provides practical and proven for creating a positive learning environment for Hispanics students.

The Light in Their Eyes: Creating Multicultural Learning Communities, Multicultural Education Series (1999)
Sonia Nieto

Sonia Nieto has been recognized numerous times for her well written, thoughtful books pertaining to multicultural education. This book not only explains what multicultural education is but describes what it looks like. In this book, Sonia Nieto clearly helps the reader understand what it takes to teach in a multicultural setting. The book is entertaining as well as informative and assists the readers in understanding what is needed to become a teacher in a multicultural setting.

Subtractive Schooling: U.S. Mexican Youth and the Politics of Caring (1999)
Angela Valenzuela

Angela Valenzuela received the Outstanding Book Award for her book entitled *Subtractive Schooling: U.S. Mexican Youth and the Politics of Caring* at the American Educational Research Association's annual meeting. It takes a provocative cluster of issues in American education—race, power, and language—beyond the usual rhetoric and adopts a fresh and thoughtful perspective. It also uses a complex array of methodological tools to address a complex issue. Most important, the voice of the researcher is clear, strong, and compelling.

We Can't Teach What We Don't Know: White Teachers, Multiracial Schools (1999)
Gary R. Howard

This is an excellent book for educators who are going to work with any culture of color. Ninety percent of teachers in this country are white. Howard's book meets a definite need in the educational community. Seamlessly combining his own experiences with the most current race/ethnicity theory, the author helps whites understand that they also have an ethnicity, and how that influences our ability to teach. Step by step, he illustrates what whites can expect as they begin to discover their own cultural identity. While this experience is often an uncomfortable one, he shows that it is possible to acknowledge responsibility for oppression of other groups without basing one's identity solely on guilt and he deals candidly with the issue of white privilege.

History

Chicano! The History of the Mexican American Civil Rights Movement, 2nd ed. (1997)
Francisco A. Rosales

Produced in conjunction with the four-part Public Broadcasting Service series of the same name, this history details the struggles of the Mexican-American community for equality and identity. It focuses on land, labor, educational reform, and political government, presenting history in the context of these themes for a broad general audience. The volume features clean page design, some black and white photos, a bibliography, and a chronology.

En Aquel Entonces (In Years Gone By): Readings in Mexican-American History (2001)
Manuel G. Gonzales and Cynthia M. Gonzales (Eds.)

Much of this work in Mexican-American history first appeared in scholarly reviews, many of them difficult to access, even among academics. This anthology of 31 articles represents a variety of disciplines on diverse aspects of the Mexican-American experience and provides a panoramic portrait of Mexicanos in the United States while at the same time introducing students to Chicana/o historiography.

The Fight in the Fields: Cesar Chavez and the Farmworkers Movement (1998)
Susan Ferriss, Ricardo Sandoval, and Diana Hembree (Eds.)

Cesar Chavez, the founder of the United Farm Workers union, was a man of principles and piety, dedicated as Gandhi and Martin Luther King Jr. were to strategies of nonviolent protest. Still controversial, Chavez is, nonetheless, beginning to fade from our collective consciousness.

Harvest of Empire: A History of Latinos in America (2001)
Juan Gonzalez

Gonzalez, a columnist for the New York Daily News, studies these latest arrivals in a book that combines history and journalism. He has a keen understanding of Hispanic diversity, focusing not just on "Hispanics" as a monolithic category but as a variety of people from many nations. The politics in *Harvest of Empire* are often tendentious.

Mexicanos: A History of Mexicans in the United States (2001)
Manuel G. Gonzales

Gonzales, a history professor at Diablo State College, anticipates controversy over his new survey of Mexican-American history. Over the past generation, that history has to a large extent been told from the perspective of the Chicano movement, with an emphasis on victimization and resistance. Gonzales aims for greater "objectivity." For example, he believes that the "Indian and the Spanish are equally important in explaining the rise of Mexican culture," and he seeks to balance accomplishments and oppression. One consequence of this approach is that Gonzales gives more credit to the more conservative groups within the Mexican-American community than some activist-scholars would.

North to Aztlan: A History of Mexican Americans in the United States (Immigrant Heritage of America Series) (1997)
Richard Griswold del Castillo and Arnoldo de León

In this extensive and comprehensive survey, Richard Griswold del Castillo and Arnoldo de León explore the complex process of cultural and economic exchange between Mexican Americans, Mexican immigrants, and a racially and ethnically diverse North American society. Examining the acculturation, work, and social patterns of Mexican Americans, the authors focus on the four primary areas of settlement: Texas, Arizona, New Mexico–Southern Colorado, and California. The history of labor and unionization, particularly the landmark achievements of the United Farm Works under Caesar Chavez, are given detailed coverage, as are the sweeping social, cultural, and intellectual changes that accompanied the emergence of the Chicano Movement of the 1960s and 1970s.

Occupied America: A History of Chicanos, 4th ed. (1999)
Rodolfo F. Acuna and Rodolfo Acuuna

Every view that we will ever see about history is skewed by personal feelings. It is our job to figure out what is fact and what is feeling. This book may not be the most objective book about the history of the Xicano people; however, it presents an important perspective.

Culture

Americanos: Latino Life in the United States (1990)
Edward James Olmos, Lea Ybarra, Manuel Monterrey, and Carlos Fuentes (Eds.)

This spirited bilingual book accomplishes a rare feat—through stirring photographs and rich text, it captures the full spectrum of Latino life in the United States. It is a socially important book. *Americanos* forces us (gently) to reevaluate, reconsider, and reestablish the very important fact that Latinos have been an integral part of the history of the United States. "The face of America should include us," Edward James Olmos asserts in his preface, and it takes but a few moments glancing at these well-rendered photographs to recognize that "face" in all its diversity.

Chicanos in a Changing Society: From Mexican Pueblos to American Barrios in Santa Barbara and Southern California, 1848–1930 (1996)
Albert Camarillo

In this book, the author sets out to provide a basis for the better understanding of a culture of people that have greatly shaped Southern California. Camarillo provides a history of the Mexican experience in Santa Barbara and other southern California cities. He begins with the U.S. annexation of California in 1848 and ends in 1930 with the deportation or "repatriation" of Mexican immigrants. Camarillo explores many aspects of the Californio and the immigrant settler and includes information on political, racial, and economical issues. This book truly provides excellent information and helps fill the gap in the one sided American history that we were taught in school.

Drink Cultura: Chicanismo (1993)
Jose Antonio Burciaga

In this collection of essays, Chicano writer Burciaga explores from Mexican-American and Chicano viewpoints the complexities of being Mexican American. Many of the essays tell of the early days of the Chicano movement in Texas, which Burciaga experienced as a child. Burciaga seeks the roots of his Chicano heritage in Mexico and Texas, telling today's Mexican Americans how the Chicano movement has changed their lives for the better. His personal anecdotes of growing up a stranger to both of his native lands speak to today's immigrants, especially the second and third generations.

Everything You Need to Know about Latino History (1998)
Himilce Novas

This book provides a historical overview of Latin American countries. Although each country is allotted only one chapter, it is surprisingly comprehensive. While it is not an in-depth coverage, it provides the reader with basic introductory material. One of the strengths of this book is that it allows the reader to compare and contrast the history of several countries that have had many common experiences.

Growing Up Chicana/o (1993)
Tiffany Anna Lopez

This is a delightful book of short stories written by a number of Hispanic authors about their childhood experiences. It examines how their experiences differed from those of the white, mainstream society and in a charming manner, the problems and the pleasures of growing up Chicana/o.

Handbook of Hispanic Cultures in the United States: Literature and Art (1993)
Alfredo Jimenez, Francisco Lomeli, and Claudia Esteve-Gabregat (Eds.)

This work focuses on the culture of Hispanics, the fastest-growing ethnic group in the United States. Reference works on Hispanic culture are few, yet this group is exerting an increasingly stronger influence on all aspects of American life. This four-volume work covering history, literature, art, anthropology, and sociology is the result. Each volume is edited by a distinguished scholar of Hispanic culture and involves the collaboration of scholars on both sides of the Atlantic.

The Hispanic Condition: Reflections on Culture and Identity in America (1996)
Ilan Stevans

Exploring history and literature to understand backgrounds (in Puerto Rico, Cuba, and Mexico) and attitudes (on race, machismo, and homosexuality, for instance) of ethnic groups, *The Hispanic Condition* insists that the focus of attention should not be Latinos as yet another immigrant group in the long succession of U.S. immigrant groups but "the hyphen" itself: the centuries-long, hemispheric "encounter between Anglos and Hispanics," an interaction in which assimilation and change flow in both directions.

Hispanic Nation: Culture, Politics, and the Constructing of Identity (1997)
Geoffrey E. Fox

Fox has done field work in Latin America, worked as a community organizer, teacher, and researcher in Puerto Rico, Chicago, and New York City, and written studies about relations between Anglo and Hispanic Americans. *Hispanic Nation* explores many factors, from media and culture to local and national politics, drawing Americans with roots in Central or South America or the Caribbean to recognize themselves as "Hispanics" and involve themselves in shaping the meaning, agenda, and place of Hispanics at the political table of those who share this identity.

Latinos: A Biography of the People (2001)
Earl Shorris

Latinos is a powerful, beautifully written, and thoughtful book, likely to remain unequaled in its sweep and profundity for some time to come. This is a smart, perceptive, and wonderfully readable book and should be required reading for anyone who would hope to understand these populations.

Hispanic Families

Becoming Mexican American: Ethnicity, Culture and Identity in Chicano Los Angeles, 1900–1945 (1995)
George J. Sanchez, Ricardo Penaranda, and Charles Bergquist (Eds.)

Los Angeles in the twentieth century is the focus of a study that deals with Mexican immigrants from 1900 to 1945. The social impact of legal and illegal immigrants and the changing ethnic makeup of Chicano communities in Los Angeles makes for an unusual study on changing American values and issues.

Con Respeto: Bridging the Distances between Culturally Diverse Families and Schools, An Ethnographic Portrait (1996)
Guadalupe Valdez

This books presents a study of ten Mexican-American families, with a special focus on how such families go about the business of surviving and learning to succeed in a new world. One of the factors that Guadalupe Valdez examines is the relationship between these families and schools. This book will help the reader develop a better understanding of the complexities poor Mexican-American families.

En mi familia (In My Family) (Children's book, 2000)
Carmen Lomas Garza (Illustrator)

Although this is a children's book it is valuable to readers of any age who are interested in Mexican American families. Garza uses her narrative paintings to relate her memories of growing up in Kingsville, Texas, near the Mexican border, and to reflect her pride in her Mexican American heritage. The artist portrays everyday events as well as special moments of family history in crisply colorful, vibrantly peopled paintings, and brief, bilingual background stories for each of the 13 paintings. Another sparkling family album that lovingly shares the artist's memories of the Hispanic cultural experience as lived in the Southwest.

Children's Books

Abuela's Weave (1993) by Omar S. Castaneda, Enrique O. Sanchez (Illustrator)
Lee & Low Books Inc., ISBN: 1880000202

Alejandro's Gift (1994) by Richard E. Albert, Sylvia Long (Illustrator)
Chronicle Books, ISBN: 0811813428

Americanos: Latino Life in the United States (1999) by Edward James Olmos
Little, Brown and Company, ISBN: 0316649090

Anita's Choice (1971) by Dorothy Hamilton, Ivan Moon (Illustrator)
Herald Press, ISBN: 0836117417/195
Reading Level: 4–8

The Black Pearl (1967) by Scott O'Dell
Dell Publishing, ISBN: 0440908035
Reading Level: 5–12

Calling the Doves (1995) by Juan Felipe Herrera, Elly Simmons (Illustrator)
Children's Book Press, ISBN: 0892391324

A Chair for My Mother (1982) by Vera B. Williams
Mulberry Paperback Books, ISBN: 0688040748

Chucaro: Wild Pony of the Pampa (1958) by Francis Kalnay, Julian de Miskey (Illustrator)
Troll Associates, ISBN: 0802773877

Cinco de Mayo (1993) by Janet Riehecky, Krystyna Stasiak (Illustrator)
Children's Book Press, ISBN: 0516406817

The Cities of Ancient Mexico Reconstructing a Lost World (1989) by Jeremy A. Sabloff, Macduff Everton (Special Photography)
Thames and Hudson, ISBN: 0500050538

Como crece una semilla (1960) by Helene J. Jordan, Loretta Krupinski (Illustrator)
Harper Arco Iris, ISBN: 0060262273
Reading Level: 1–2

The Corn Grows Ripe (1956, 1984) by Dorothy Rhoads, Jean Charlot (Illustrator)
Penguin Books, ISBN: 0140363130
Reading Level: Ages 8–12

The Crossing (1987) by Gary Paulsen
Bantam Doubleday Dell Books for Young Readers, ISBN: 0440205824
Reading Level: 7

Diego (1991) by Jonah Winter, Jeanette Winter (Illustrator)
Dragonfly Books, ISBN: 067985617X

Donde viven los monstruos (1963, 1991) by Maurice Sendak
HarperTrophy, ISBN: 0064434222

El conejito andarin (Audio book) (1972) by Margaret Wise Brown, Clement Hurd (Illustrator)
Harper Arco Iris, ISBN: 069470024X

El Día de los Muertos (1997) by Tony Johnston, Jeanette Winter (Illustrator)
Mariuccia Iaconi, ISBN: 0962872042

El esqueleto dentro de ti (1971) by Philip Balestrino, True Kelley (Illustrator)
Harper Arco Iris, ISBN: 0064451445
Reading Level: Ages 5–9

El gran ganero rojo (1984) by Maragret Wise Brown, Felicia Bond (Illustrator)
Harper Arco Iris, ISBN: 0060262257

Erandi's Braids (1999) by Antonio Hernandez Madrigal, Tomie dePaola (Illustrator)
Scholastic Inc., ISBN: 0439168406
Reading Level: K–4

Family Pictures-Cuadros de familia (1990) by Carmen Lomas Garza (Illustrator)
Children's Book Press, ISBN: 0892391081
Reading Level: K–6

The Farolitos of Christmas (1987) by Rudolfo Anaya, Deward Gonzales (Illustrator)
Hypervision Books for Children, ISBN: 0786800607

Felita (1979) by Nicholosa Mohr, Ray Cruz (Illustrator)
Bantam Doubleday Dell Books for Young Readers, ISBN: 0440412951
Reading Level: 4

Friends from the Other Side (1993) by Gloria Anzaldua, Consuelo Mendez (Illustrator)
Children's Book Press, ISBN: 0892391308

A Gift for Tia Rosa (1986) by Karen T. Taha, Dee deRosa (Illustrator)
Bantam Skylark Books, ISBN: 055315978X
Reading Level: 3

Going Home (1986) by Nicholasa Mohr
Bantam Skylark Books, ISBN: 0553156993
Reading Level: 6

Grandmother's Adobe Dollhouse (1984) by MaryLou M. Smith, Ann Blackstone (Illustrator)
New Mexico Magazine, ISBN: 0937206075

The Gullywasher (1995) by Joyce Rossi (Illustrator)
Northland Publishing, ISBN: 0873586077

Harry: el perrito sucio (1956,1984) by Gene Zion, Margaret Bloy Graham (Illustrator)
Harper Arco Iris, ISBN: 0060270527
Reading Level: Ages 4–8

The Honorable Prison (1988) by Lyll Becerra de Jenkins
Puffin Books, ISBN: 0140329528
Reading Level: Ages 12 and up

House of Adobe (1995) by Bonnie Shemie
Tundra Books, ISBN: 0887763537

Iktomi and the Boulder (1988) by Paul Goble (Illustrator)
The Trumpet Club, ISBN: 0440847583

In My Family (1996) by Carmen Lomas Garza (Illustrator)
Children's Book Press, ISBN: 0892391383

In the Barrio (1994) by Alma Flor Ada, Liliana Wilson Grez (Illustrator)
Scholastic Inc., ISBN: 0590275690

The Invisible Hunters (1997) by Harriet Rhomer, Joe Sam (Illustrator)
Children's Book Press, ISBN: 0892390549
Reading Level: 3

I Speak English for My Mom (1989) by Muriel Stanek, Judith Friedman (Illustrator)
Albert Whitman & Company, ISBN: 0807536598

It Doesn't Have to Be This Way (1999) by Luis J. Rodriguez, Daniel Galvez (Illustrator)
Children's Book Press, ISBN: 0892391618

Jalapeno Bagels (1996) by Natasha Wing, Robert Casilla (Illustrator)
Atheneum Books for Young Readers, ISBN: 0689805306
Reading Level: Ages 5–8

Josefina y la colcha de retazos (Audio book) (1986) by Eleanor Coerr, Bruce Degen (Illustrator)
Harper Arco Iris, ISBN: 0694700231

Kids Explore America's Hispanic Heritage (1994) by Rob Crisell, Peggy Shaefer, and Elizabeth Wolf (Eds.)
John Muir Publications, ISBN: 1562612727

Kingdoms of Gold, Kingdoms of Jade: The Americas before Columbus (1991) by Brian M. Fagan
Thames and Hudson, ISBN: 0500050627

Living up the Street (1985) by Gary Soto
Bantam Doubleday Dell Books for Young Readers, ISBN: 0440211700
Reading Level: 6

Lupita Mañana (1981) by Particia Beatty
Beech Tree Books, ISBN: 0688114970
Reading Level: Ages 12 and up

Maria: A Christmas Story (1992) by Theodore Taylor
Avon Camelot Books, ISBN: 0380721201
Reading Level: 5.4

My Name Is Maria Isabel (1993) by Alma Flor Ada, K. Dyble Thompson (Illustrator)
Aladdin Paperbacks, ISBN: 068980217X
Reading Level: ages 7–10

My House: A Book in Two Languages (1990) by Rebecca Emberly (Illustrator)
Little, Brown and Company, ISBN: 0316234486

The New True Book: The Maya (1985) by Patricia C. McKissack
Childrens Press, ISBN: 0516412701

Nine Days to Christmas: A Story of Mexico (1959) by Marie Hall Ets, and Aurora Labastida, Marie Hall Ets (Illustrator)
The Viking Press, ISBN: 0833578642

Old Ramon (1960, 1988) by Jack Shaefer, Harold West (Illustrator)
Troll Associates, ISBN: 0802774032
Reading Level: 6–8

Pablo and Pimienta (1993) by Ruth M. Covault, Francisco Mora (Illustrator)
Rising Moon, ISBN: 0873587081

Parrot in the Oven (1996) by Victor Martinez
HarperTrophy, ISBN: 0064471861
Reading Level: 7–8

A Picture Book of Simón Bolívar (1992) by David A. Adler, Robert Castilla (Illustrator)
Scholastic Inc., ISBN: 0590470167
Reading Level: Ages 4–8

The Piñata Maker (1994) by George Ancona
Harcourt Brace & Company, ISBN: 0152000607

Pumpkin Fiesta (1998) by Caryn Yacowitz, Joe Cepeda (Illustrator)
HarperCollins Publishers, ISBN: 0060276584
Reading Level: Ages 3–6

Radio Man (1993) by Arthur Dorros (Illustrator)
HarperCollins Publishers, ISBN: 006021547X
Reading Level: K–4

Rain Player (1991) by David Wisniewski
Clarion Books, ISBN: 0395551129

Rio Grande Stories (1994) by Carolyn Meyer
Harcourt Brace & Company, ISBN: 0152000666
Reading Level: Ages 10–14

Roberto Clemente, All-Star Hero (1991) by Jim O'Connor, Stephen Marchesi (Illustrator)
Dell Publishing, ISBN: 0440912792
Reading Level: 3–4

Say Hola, Sarah (1995) by Patricia Reilly Giff, DyAnne DiSalvo-Ryan (Illustrator)
Bantam Doubleday Dell Books for Young Readers, ISBN: 0440911885
Reading Level: 2–3

Sees Behind Trees (1996) by Michael Dorris
Scholastic Inc., ISBN: 0590108514
Reading Level: 8–12

Se Venden Gorras (1940) by Esphyr Slobodkina
Harper Arco Iris, ISBN: 006443401X
Reading Level: Ages 4–7

Si le das una galletita a un ratón (1985) by Laura Joffe Numeroff, Felicia Bond (Illustrator)
Harper Arco Iris, ISBN: 0060254386
Reading Level: Ages 3–7

Si le das un panqueque a una cerdita (1998) by Laura Numeroff, Felicia Bond (Illustrator)
Harper Arco Iris, ISBN: 0060283165
Reading Level: Ages 3–7

The Sombrero of Luis Lucero (1993) by Cecilia Avalos, Larry Raymond (Illustrator)

Sundance Publishers and Distributors, ISBN: 1568010591

Spirits of the High Mesa (1997) by Floyd Martinez, Consuelo Udave (Illustrator)
Arte Publico Press, ISBN: 1558851984

Sweet Fifteen (1995) by Diane Gonzales Bertrand, Gladys Ramirez (Cover Art)
Pinata Books, ISBN: 155885133X
Reading Level: 7–10

The Tamarindo Puppy (1980) by Charlotte Pomerantz, Byron Barton (Illustrator)
Mulberry Books, ISBN: 0688115144

Tomás and the Library Lady (1997) by Pat Mora, Raul Colon (Illustrator)
Alfred A. Knopf, ISBN: 0679804013

Too Many Tamales (1993) by Gary Soto, Ed Martinez (Illustrator)
The Putnam and Grosset Group, ISBN: 0698114124

The Tortilla Factory (1995) by Gary Paulsen, Ruth Wright Paulsen (Illustrator)
Harcourt Brace and Company: Voyager Books, ISBN: 0152928766

Tortilla for Emilia (1992) by Maria Angeles, Carol Newsom (Illustrator)
Sundance Publishing, ISBN: 0887419291

The Tortilla Quilt (1996) by Jane Tenorio-Coscarelli (Illustrator)
¼Inch Publishing, ISBN: 0965342212

Trino's Choice (1994) by Diane Gonzales Bertrand
Piñata Books, ISBN: 0558852689

Vejigantes masquerade (1993) by Lulu Delacre
Scholastic Inc., ISBN: 0590457772
Reading Level: Ages 5–9

Viva México! A Story of Benito Juárez and Cinco de Mayo (1993) by Argentina Palacios, Howard Berelson (Illustrator)
Steck-Vaughn Company, ISBN: 0811480542

Where Angels Glide at Dawn (1990) Lori M. Carlson and Cynthia L. Ventura (Eds.), Jose Ortega (Illustrator)
HarperTrophy, ISBN: 0064404641
Reading Level: Ages 10 and up

Adult Fiction

These are some of our favorites to read for enjoyment, although we learned a great deal about various cultural beliefs and practices in the process.

Books

Bless Me, Ultima, by Rudolfo A. Anaya

Dominoes and Other Stories from the Puerto Rican, by Jack Agueros

Dona Flora and Her Two Husbands, by Jorge Amando

Dreaming in Cuban, by Cristina Garcia

Happy Birthday, Jesús, by Ronald L. Ruiz

The House on Mango Street, by Sandra Cisneros

The Infinite Plan, by Isabel Allende

In Search of Snow, by Luis Alberto Urrea

In the Time of the Butterflies, by Julia Alvarez

The Killing of Saints, by Alex Abella

Like Water for Chocolate, by Laura Esquivel

The Lonely Crossing of Juan Cabrera, by J. Joaquin Fraxedas

The Mambo Kings Play Songs of Love, by Oscar Hijuelos

Mirrors Beneath the Earth: Short Fiction, by Chicano Writers

Santiago and the Drinking Party, by Clay Morgan

Short Fiction by Hispanic Writers of the United States

So Far from Home, by Ana Castillo

Spidertown, by Abraham Rodriquez

Movies about Hispanics

Title: *El Norte*

Topic: Trials of two illegal immigrants

Description: Beginning in the remote mountain jungles of Guatemala, this drama about a brother and sister seeking a better life centers on two young Indians. When the father is killed and their mother is taken away, they set off for the "promise land" to the north—El Norte. When they finally reach Los Angeles their trials are not yet over. They are "illegals" submerged in an alien culture.

Title: *The Mission*

Cast: Robert DeNiro, Jeremy Irons

Date: 1986

Description: The story of a man of the cloth and a man of the sword who unite to shield a South American Indian tribe from brutal subjugation by eighteenth century colonial empires. A clash of wills and cultures.

Title: *Milagro Beanfield War*

Cast: Ruben Blades, Richard Bradford, Sonia Braga

Date: 1988

Description: When a Chicano handyman from the Milagro Valley decides to irrigate his small beanfield by "borrowing" some water from a large development site, he sets off a chain reaction that results in a culture clash.

Title: *My Family*

Topic: Three generation of a Mexican American family and their stories in America

Cast: Jimmy Smits, Esai Morales

Date: 1995

Description: This is a story about the Sanchez family as told by their eldest son. From the beginning of his father's adventurous journey from Mexico to California in the 1920s to the present. (Academy Award Winner)

Title: *The Old Gringo*

Cast: Jane Fonda, Gregory Peck, Jimmy Smits

A spinster American schoolteacher travels to a hacienda in Mexico to teach the children of a wealthy landowner. What she finds is that she is in the midst of the Mexican Revolution. The three main characters are a a general in Pancho Villa's Revolutionary Army, a journalist (Ambrose Bierce, who disappeared in Mexico in 1913), and the school teacher. Based on Carlos Fuentes' novel.

Title: *Stand and Deliver*

Cast: James Edward Olmos, Lou Diamond Phillips

A Hispanic mathematics teacher holds Latino high school students to high expectations by insisting they are able to learn calculus. Students rise to the occasion by studying extra hours and helping each other. The teacher's unorthodox methods and strong belief in the students' abilities are models for other teachers of Hispanic students.

Title: *A Walk in the Clouds*

Cast: Keanu Reeves

Date: 1996

Description: Wealthy Mexican American family of three generations and their joys and problems. Takes place in the late 1940s and is the story of young woman who is pregnant and is afraid her traditional father will turn her away.

Videos about Hispanics

Library Video

www.libraryvideo.com

The Hispanic American Experience in Fiction

www.rbls.lib.il.us/dpl/ph02969j.jpg

American Cultures for Children Video Series

Actress Phylicia Rashad warmly introduces children to the rich tapestry of world cultures thriving in America today. Each culture is presented in fun and fast-paced educational segments that celebrate the community's values and traditions. Programs include geography and history segments about the culture's original country of origin, kid-hosted tours of neighborhood restaurants, markets, and festivals, foreign language segments in which children learn to count to ten and say "hello," "goodbye," "thank you," and "friend," arts and crafts demonstrations, a traditional animated folktale and a traditional folksong performed by a chorus of children and musicians.

Caribbean Close-Up: Haiti and The Dominican Republic

28 minutes $16.95

Grades 4 to 8

In Haiti, meet Marie, a 14-year-old who lives in a fishing village. She lives with her younger sister, mother, and grandmother. Watch as the women work in poor conditions to complete their chores. In the Dominican Republic, meet Jonathan, a 13-year-old who lives with his family in a housing project. Baseball and Sammy Sosa play an important role in Jonathan's life. Visit Jonathan's school and home to gain perspective. Part of the Children of the Earth Series.

Central America Close-Up: El Salvador and Guatemala

28 minutes $16.95

Grades 4 to 8

Learn about life in other countries by following two teenagers through their daily routines. First travel to El Salvador and meet Marvin Benitez, whose family returns to their war-torn homeland and attempts to bring some stability and peace to their fractured lives in the coastal village of Nueva Esperanza. Next, travel to Guatemala and meet Natividad Hernandez, a young Maya Indian whose mountain village still carries on a very traditional way of life. The construction of a nearby roadway challenges the traditions of Hernandez and her family, foreshadowing the end of customs that haven't changed for centuries. Part of the Children of the Earth Series.

Cuba Close-Up

28 minutes $16.95

Grades 4 to 8

Meet Yudey, a 14-year-old, who lives in Pinar del Rio. Yudey hopes to take advantage of Cuba's excellent free education when she is older. Visit her school and watch as she helps her parents fire up a sawdust stove to cook dinner. Next, meet 14-year-old Eduardo who lives in Havana. Watch as Eduardo bicycles around his neighborhood, visits a farmer's market with his mom and sister, and attends a rite of Santaria with his father and brother. Part of the Children of the Earth Series.

Kids Explore Mexico

28 minutes $9.95

Grade 1 to 6

Explore the geography, history, and culture of Mexico as children take a tour of Aztec and Mayan ruins, share a meal with a Mexican family, join festive guitar players and flamenco dancers, and discover maps that lead to Mexican treasures. Part of an educational multi-volume series.

Mexican-American Heritage

25 minutes $29.95

Grades K to 4

[Schlessinger Media]

Mexico's intriguing history, culture, and landscape are illuminated in this program about the life and heritage of Mexican Americans. Children learn how to say a few words in Spanish; take a tour of the Olvera Street market in Los Angeles, the oldest Mexican-American market in the United States; and learn how to make a colorful yarn painting. They'll also enjoy an animated folktale called "The Great Race," and sing along with the chorus to the Mexican folksong, "Cielito Lindo," which means "beautiful sky." Part of the American Cultures for Children Video Series, introducing children to the rich tapestry of world cultures thriving in America today.

Mexican Americans

30 minutes $39.95

Grades 4 to 10

[Schlessinger Media]

Four hundred years ago, Spanish explorers enslaved the Aztec, an advanced native society living in Mexico. Together, the Spanish and Aztec became farmers until the Mexican-American War resulted in large amounts of Mexican land being claimed by the United States. Approximately 80 percent of the Mexicans became U.S. citizens. By the turn of the century, the railroad and mining industries relied heavily on Mexican-American labor. The United States continues to be shaped by the values, customs, and hard work of Mexican Americans. Their continued success and acceptance further blurs the line between what is called "Mexican" and what is considered "American." Part of a compelling series that celebrates the heritage of different cultural groups in North America.

Mexico's Day of the Dead

$29.95

Grades 4 to 8

This program places Mexico's Day of the Dead in a cultural context and traces the history of the celebration. It also looks at the art and preparations associated with the holiday. Features 16 craft projects, a visit with folk artists in the marketplace, an interactive tour of a Mexican village, a visit to a Mexican home in preparation for the holiday and more. In Spanish and English. (Bilingual Spanish/English)

Puerto Rican Heritage

25 minutes $29.95

Grades K to 4

[Schlessinger Media]

Exciting adventures appear at every turn as children are introduced to the U.S. Commonwealth of Puerto Rico and learn about Puerto Ricans who have come to live on the U.S. mainland, bringing their unique cultural traditions with them. Everyone learns to count to ten and say a few words in Spanish. Then children visit the town of Ponce, Puerto Rico, where a carnival celebration is in full swing, with parades, colorful costumes, masks, festive music and dancing. Children learn to make their own carnival mask, watch an animated folktale, "Song of the Coqui," about the native Puerto Rican frog and sing a folksong about the frog, called "El Coqui." Part of the American Cultures for Children Video Series, introducing children to the rich tapestry of world cultures thriving in America today.

Families of Mexico

30 minutes $29.95

Grades Pre-K to 4

Explore urban and rural daily life in households in Mexico through a child's point of view. Spend a day with two families and discover information about Mexican food, clothing, housing styles, religion, and education. Learn the answer to many questions about Mexican culture and develop a real feel for life in this country. Part of the Families of the World series.

Chicano! History of the Mexican American Civil Rights Movement Series

Available from the National Latino Communications Center

3171 Los Feliz Blvd. Suite 200
Los Angeles, CA 90039
323-663-8294

www.pbs.org/chicano

This is a series of videos documenting the social, economic, and political aspects of the Civil Rights Movement as it related to Mexican Americans. The video, Chicano! Taking Back the Schools, is particularly relevant to educators. It powerfully describes how students in an East Los Angeles high school demanded a more equitable education, walking out of school to dramatize their needs, and enlist parent support. Hispanics who are successful professionals today and were students in the high school in the 1960s tell their story in their own words. The juxtaposition of film showing the students in the 1960s and showing them as adults is especially poignant and compelling. The students and a few of their teachers and parents were in real danger as they courageously led the fight for civil rights for Mexican American students.

Websites

Hispanic Americans in the Humanities: 20th Century A Biographical Tour of the World Wide Web

www.ithaca.edu/library/htmls/humhisp.html

These sites contain biographical information concerning important Hispanic American personalities of the twentieth century who have made contributions to several fields within the humanities. "Humanities" is difficult to define, but to make this site more manageable, individuals from music and performing arts are not included. Leaders in civil rights and politics are omitted unless they also fit into another category (many do). At the bottom of the page are some links to other biographical sources.

Hispanic American History and Literature for K–12

http://falcon.jmu.edu/~ramseyil/hispan.htm

- Literature
- Biography
- Periodicals
- Hispanic heritage
- History Mexican Americans

Mexican History

Zapatistas

www.cs.unb.ca/~alopez-o/politics/zapatista.html

Mexican Revolution 1910

www.mexonline.com/revolution.htm

Quetzalcoatl

www.weber.ucsd.edu/~anthclub/quetzal.htm

Cinco de Mayo

www.mexonline.com/cinco.htm

Hispanic Heritage

www.sat.lib.tx.us/html/hispanic.htm

This page is devoted to websites that provide useful information on the Hispanic population of the United States. Many questions focus on the history, people, and culture of Mexico. To help answer those questions, see the Mexico and the Hispanic Heritage Month page. You will find information on Latina writers, Tejano music, Hispanic genealogy, border issues, and much more.

American Hispanics in Congress—1882–1995

www.loc.gov/rr/hispanic/congress/

This site presents a history of Hispanics in Congress providing a very interesting history as well as a short biography of those currently serving.

Republic of Cuba W.W.W.

www.unipr.it/~davide/cuba/HomePage.html

These three sites provide some very interesting, if slightly biased, information.

- CubaWeb Net–NEW
- Cuban Internet Resources by P. Klee
- Cuba, Portrait of a Nation by CubaNet

Welcome to the Caribbean Cultural Center

http://archive.nandotimes.com/prof/caribe/Caribbean_Cultural_Center.html

More than 500 years ago, three cultures met in the warmth of the Caribbean. The results emerged through music, dance, religion, literature, plastic arts, and much more, which this site shares.

National Hispanic Heritage Month

www.cr.nps.gov/NR/feature/hispanic/

The National Register of Historic Places is pleased to help foster the general public's awareness, understanding, and appreciation for Hispanic culture during National Hispanic Heritage Month. As part of the celebration, this site highlights various publications, properties listed in the National

Register, and National Parks that deal directly with the ingenuity, creativity, cultural, and political experiences of Hispanic Americans. Join the National Register of Historic Places in recognizing and exploring the achievements of a people that have contributed so much to American culture.

Civil Rights

www.nclr.org/policy/civil.html

Discrimination in employment, housing, and other aspects of daily life severely limits the economic and social opportunities available to Hispanic Americans. National Council of La Raza conducts policy analysis and advocacy activities in the civil rights arena in order to promote and protect equality of opportunity in education, employment, housing, public services, and public accommodations for all Americans.

Office of Migrant Education

www-bcf.usc.edu/~cmmr/Latino.html

The Office of Migrant Education works to improve teaching and learning for migratory children. Programs and projects administered by OME are designed to enable children whose families migrate to find work in agricultural, fishing, and timber industries to meet the same challenging academic content and student performance standards that are expected of all children. The migrant education program is based on the premise that migrant children, although affected by poverty and the migrant lifestyle can and should have the opportunity to realize their full academic potential.

Hispanics in the Military

www.csbs.utsa.edu/users/vlevva/military.htm

www.getnet.com/~1stbooks/medal2.htm

www.getnet.com/~1stbooks/unit3c.htm

www.hispaniconline.com/hh/civil war.html

www.almaproject.dpsk12.org/stories/storyReader$26

www.neta.com/~1stbooks/confed.htm

www.agif.org/longoria.html

www.dtic.mil/soldiers/sept94/p52.html

Archeology

Teotihuacan

http://archaeology.la.asu.edu/teo/

Museums
www.umco.org/espanol/index.html

Arts
www.mexicool.com/default.html

Frida Kahlo
www.fridakahlo.it/

Diego Rivera
www.diegorivera.com/index.html

Ballet Folklorico
www.ballet-folc-nal.com.mx/
www.arts-history.mx/danza/dan.html

Figures—Oaxaca
www.mexonline.com/animal1.htm

La Leyenda de la Flor de la Nochebuena
Parents' Choice Award, tells the legend of the poinsettia which grows abundantly in Mexico during Christmas time and is a favorite flower for families.

Discovering Mexico
www.nationalgeographic.com/features/96/mexico/a006.html

Magazines and Other Periodicals

El Puente
A Spanish newletter with bilingual glossary. Each 16 page issue delivers a fascinating range of articles from world news to culture. It provides practice for native speakers as well as those trying to learn Spanish for middle to high school students. To subscribe, call 800-600-4494 or visit website at www.ednews.com

Hispanic Magazine
This magazine is edited for the contemporary Hispanic and focuses on success stories that present the achievements and contributions that today's Hispanics are making to U.S. society. It also contains articles on en-

tertainment, education, business, sports, the arts, literature, politics, government, national and international personalities, and events that impact U.S. Hispanics. To get a free issue or to subscribe online, go to www.hispaniconline.com/magazine.

Críticas

An English speaker's guide to the latest Spanish language titles. Includes practical tips for serving Spanish-speaking communities, news, reviews and previews of adult and juvenile titles, plus hot new books and videos. Call 1-866-456-0401 or fax 1-818-487-4550. www.pubservice.com/cahners.htm.

INDEX